'The True
Standard Advanced',

'The Law of Freedom'

and Other Writings

Gerrard Winstanley

Copyright © introduction and this edition Will Jonson

First Edition, 2014

ISBN: 978-14992754879

All Rights reserved. No part of this publication may be reproduced, copied, stored in a retrieval system, or transmitted, in any form or by any means, without the prior written consent of the copyright holder, nor be otherwise circulated in any form of binding or cover other than that in which it is published and without a similar condition being imposed on the subsequent purchaser

CONTENTS

Introduction	5
The True Levellers' Standard Advanced	7
A Declaration from the Poor Oppressed People of England	24
A New Year's Gift for the Parliament & the Army	31
A Letter to the Lord Fairfax	52

The Law of Freedom in a Platform or True Magistracy Revealed

To His Excellency Oliver Cromwell	64
To the Friendly and Unbiased Reader	78
Chapter One	80
Chapter Two	90
Chapter Three	99
Chapter Four	108
Chapter Five	142
Chapter Six	153

INTRODUCTION

At primary school we studied the English Civil War, but very superficially, and with all the stereotyping that the dominant culture fed us through novels like *Children of the New Forest* and TV series set during the war. Because the Royalists eventually won (Charles II being restored in 1660), it was the official image that we were fed. Thus, the Royalists (while officially the 'baddies') were wild, reckless and romantic; the Parliamentarians dull, dour and boring. These images still infect and distort our culture and our representations of that era. And I was confused by the paradox of the presentation of attractive 'bad guys' and just, fair and forward-looking 'good guys' presented as villains.

In the sixth form I did History A level and learnt that real historians didn't call it 'The English Civil War'; they called it 'The English Revolution' – and that the years of the war brought an outpouring of radical ideas – many of which found themselves in print.

The Diggers were the most radical of all. Calling themselves 'True Levellers' to distinguish themselves from the Levellers (who merely wanted a vote for every man – something that would not happen in England until 1928), the Diggers proposed the abolition of private property and money. They were centuries ahead of their time.

The Diggers were led by Gerrard Winstanley (although he would have eschewed that appellation – just as Marcos is Subcomandante Marcos, subservient to the people). Winstanley's main writings are reproduced here: the first three date from 1649, 'The Law of Freedom' from 1652.

In their attempts to cultivate common land and in their ideas, they look back to Wat Tyler's Peasants' Revolt and forwards to the Occupy Movement. When I read Winstanley write 'England is a prison', I am reminded of Linton Kwesi Johnson's more recent poem 'Inglan is a Bitch'. The Diggers mounted a doomed but real experiment in egalitarian collectivization of the land – one that looks forward to

Communism and one which deserves to be read and remembered. In every word and sentence in this book a sense of injustice and unfairness burns, as does a very real way of running things better for the ordinary man and woman. One might argue that 'The Law of Freedom' is as close to a written constitution as England has ever got.

Of course, the Diggers were ruthlessly crushed by Cromwell's soldiers, and the status quo was maintained. But their ideas – and the injustices which lad to them – still live on.

Will Jonson

London, January 2014.

A note on the text:

In the main titles, I have changed Winstanley's spelling and punctuation to conform to modern usage – perhaps that was wrong: after all, what's an apostrophe, when you're fighting for a revolution? In the main texts I have left Winstanley's spelling and punctuation untouched, since it preserves a flavor of the time and does not impede the reader's understanding.

The True Levellers' Standard Advanced: or, The State of Community Opened, and Presented to the Sons of Men

A Declaration to the Powers of England, and to all the Powers of the World, shewing the Cause why the Common People of England have begun, and gives Consent to Digge up, Manure, and Sow Corn upon George-Hill in Surrey; by those that have Subscribed, and thousands more that gives Consent.

In the beginning of Time, the great Creator Reason, made the Earth to be a Common Treasury, to preserve Beasts, Birds, Fishes, and Man, the lord that was to govern this Creation; for Man had Domination given to him, over the Beasts, Birds, and Fishes; but not one word was spoken in the beginning, That one branch of mankind should rule over another.

And the Reason is this, Every single man, Male and Female, is a perfect Creature of himself; and the same Spirit that made the Globe, dwels in man to govern the Globe; so that the flesh of man being subject to Reason, his Maker, hath him to be his Teacher and Ruler within himself, therefore needs not run abroad after any Teacher and Ruler without him, for he needs not that any man should teach him, for the same Anoynting that ruled in the Son of man, teacheth him all things.

But since humane flesh (that king of Beasts) began to delight himself in the objects of the Creation, more then in the Spirit Reason and Righteosness, who manifests himself to be the indweller in the Five Sences, of Hearing, Seeing, Tasting, Smelling, Feeling; then he fell into blindness of mind and weakness of heart, and runs abroad for a Teacher and Ruler: And so selfish imaginations taking possession of the Five Sences, and ruling as King in the room of Reason therein, and working with Covetousnesse, did set up one man to teach and rule over another; and thereby the Spirit was killed, and man was brought into bondage, and became a greater Slave to such of his own kind, then the Beasts of the field were to him.

And hereupon, The Earth (which was made to be a Common Treasury of relief for all, both Beasts and Men) was hedged in to In-closures by the teachers and rulers, and the others were made Servants and Slaves: And that Earth that is within this Creation made a Common Store-house for all, is bought and sold, and kept in the hands of a few, whereby the great Creator is mightily dishonoured, as if he were a respector of persons, delighting int he comfortable Livelihoods of some, and rejoycing in the miserable povertie and straits of others. From the beginning it was not so.

But this coming in of Bondage, is called "A-dam", because this ruling and teaching power without, doth "dam" up the Spirit of Peace and Liberty; First within the heart, by filling it with slavish fears of others. Secondly without, by giving the bodies of one to be imprisoned, punished and oppressed by the outward power of another. And this evil was brought upon us through his own Covetousnesse, whereby he is blinded and made weak, and sees not the Law of Righteousnesse in his heart, which is the pure light of Reason, but looks abroad for it, and thereby the Creation is cast under bondage and curse, and the creator is sleighted; First by the Teachers and Rulers that sets themselves down in the Spirits room, to teach and rule, where he himself is only King. Secondly by the other, that refuses the Spirit, to be taught and governed by fellow Creatures, and this was called Israels Sin, in casting off the Lord and chusing Saul, one like themselves to be their King, when as they had the same Spirit of Reason and government in themselves, as he had, if they were but subject. And Israels rejecting of outward teachers and rulers to embrace the Lord, and to be all taught and ruled by that righteous King, that Jeremiah Prophesied shall rule in the new Heavens and new Earth in the latter dayes, will be their Restauration from bondage, Jer. 23.5, 6.

But for the present state of the old World that is running up like parchment in the fire, and wearing away, we see proud Imaginary flesh, which is the wise Serpent, rises up in flesh and gets dominion in some to rule over others, and so forces one part of the Creation man, to be a slave to another; and thereby the Spirit is killed in both. The one looks upon himself as a teacher and ruler, and so is lifted up in pride over his fellow Creature: The other looks upon himself as imperfect, and so is dejected in his spirit, and looks upon his fellow Creature of his own Image, as a Lord above him.

And thus Esau, the man of flesh, which is Covetousness and Pride, hath killed Jacob, the Spirit of meeknesse, and righteous government in the light of Reason, and rules over him: And so the Earth that was made a common Treasury for all to live comfortably upon, is become through mans unrighteous actions one over another, to be a place, wherein one torments another.

Now the great Creator, who is the Spirit Reason, suffered himself thus to be rejected, and troden underfoot by the covetous proud flesh, for a certain time limited; therefore saith he, The Seed out of whom the Creation did proceed, which is my Self, shall bruise this Serpents head, and restore my Creation again from this curse and bondage; and when I the King of Righteousnesse raigns in every man, I will be the blessing of the Earth and the joy of all Nations.

And since the coming in of the stoppage, or the A-dam the Earth hath been inclosed and given to the Elder brother Esau, or man of flesh, and hath been bought and sold from one to another; and Jacob, or the younger brother, that is to succeed or come forth next, who is the universal spreading power of righteousnesse that gives liberty to the whole Creation, is made a servant.

And this Elder Son, or man of bondage, hath held the Earth in bondage to himself, not by a meek Law of Righteousnesse, But by subtle selfish Councels, and by open and violent force; for wherefore is it that there is such Wars and rumours of Wars in the Nations of the Earth? and wherefore are men so mad to destroy one another? But only to uphold Civil propriety of Honor, Dominion and Riches one over another, which is the curse the Creation groans under, waiting for deliverance.

But when once the Earth becomes a Common Treasury again, as it must, for all the Prophesies of Scriptures and Reason are Circled here in this Community, and mankind must have the Law of Righteousness once more writ in his heart, and all must be made of one heart, and one mind.

Then this Enmity in all Lands will cease, for none shall dare to seek a Dominion over others, neither shall any dare to kill another, nor desire more of the Earth then another; for he that will rule over, imprison, oppresse, and kill his fellow Creatures, under what pretence soever, is a destroyer of the Creation, and an actor of the Curse, and walks contrary to the rule of righteousnesse: (Do, as you would have others do to you; and love your Enemies, not in words, but in actions).

Therefore you powers of the Earth, or Lord Esau, the Elder brother, because youy have appeared to rule the Creation, first take notice, That the powere that sets you to work, is selvish Covetousness, and an aspiring Pride, to live in glory and ease over Jacob, the meek Spirit; that is, the Seed that lies hid, in & among the poor Common People, or younger Brother, out of whom the blessing of Deliverance is to rise and spring up to all Nations.

And Reason, the living king of righteousnesse, doth only look on, and lets thee alone, That whereas thou counts thy self an Angel of Light, thou shalt appear in the light of the Sun, to be a Devil, A-dam, and the Curse that the Creation groans under; and the time is now come for thy downfal, and Jacob must rise, who is the universal Spirit of love and righteousnesse, that fils, and will fill all the Earth.

Thou teaching and ruling power of flesh, thou hast had three periods of time, to vaunt thy self over thy Brother; the first was from the time of thy coming in, called A-dam, or a stoppage, till Moses came; and there thou that wast a self-lover in Cain, killed thy brother Abel, a plain-hearted man that loved righteousnesse: And thou by thy wisdom and beastly government, made the whole Earth to stinck, till Noah came, which was a time of the world, like the coming in of the watery Seed into the womb, towards the bringing forth of the man child.

And from Noah till Moses came, thou still hast ruled in vaunting, pride, and cruel oppression; Ishmael against Isaac, Esau against Jacob; for thou hast still been the man of flesh that hath ever persecuted the man of righteousnesse, the Spirit Reason.

And Secondly, from Moses till the Son of Man came, which was time of the world, that the man child could not speak like a man, but lisping, making signs to shew his meaning; as we see many Creatures that cannot speak do. For Moses Law was a Language lapped up in Types, Sacrifices, Forms, and Customs, which was weak time. And in this time likewise, O thou teaching and ruling power, thou wast an oppressor; for look into Scriptures and see if Aaron and the Priests were not the first that deceived the people; and the Rulers, as Kings and Governors, were continually the Ocean-head, out of whose power, Burdens, Oppressions, and Poverty did flow out upon the Earth: and these two Powers still hath been the Curse, that hath led the Earth, mankind, into confusion and death by their imaginary and selvish teaching and ruling, and it could be no otherwise; for while man looks upon himself, as an imperfect Creation, and seeks and runs abroad for a teacher and a rule, he is all this time a stranger to the Spirit that is within himself.

But though the Earth hath been generally thus in darknesse, since the A-dam rise up, and hath owned a Light, and a Law without them to walk by, yet some have been found as watchmen, in this night time of the world, that have been taught by the Spirit within them, and not by any flesh without them, as Abraham, Isaac, Jacob, and the Prophets: And these, and such as these, have still been the Butt, at whom, the powers of the Earth in all ages of the world, by their selvish Laws, have shot their fury.

And then Thirdly, from the time of the Son of man, which was time that the man-child began to speak like a child growing upward to manhood, till now, that the Spirit is rising up in strength. O thou teaching and ruling power of the earthly man, thou has been an oppressor, by imprisonment, impoverishing, and martyrdom; and all thy power and wit, hath been to make Laws, and execute thm against such as stand for universal Liberty, which is the rising up of Jacob: as by those ancient enslaving Laws not yet blotted out, but held up as weapons against the man-child.

O thou Powers of England, though thou hast promised to make this People a Free People, yet thou hast so handled the matter, through thy self-seeking humour, That thou has wrapped us up more in bondage, and oppression lies heavier upon us; not only bringing thy fellow Creatures, the Commoners, to a morsel of Bread, but by confounding all sorts of people by thy Government, of doing and undoing.

First, Thou hast made the people to take a Covenant and Oaths to endeavour a Reformation, and to bring in Liberty every man in his place; and yet while a man is in pursuing of that Covenant, he is imprisoned and oppressed by thy Officers, Courts, and Justices, so called.

critique of the social contract.

Think about the 'atmosphere' of ideology (Althusser) + political institutions.

Thou hast made Ordinances to cast down Oppressing, Popish, Episcopal, Self-willed and Prerogative Laws; yet we see, That Self-wil and Prerogative power, is the great standing Law, that rules all in action, and others in words.

Thou hast made many promises and protestations to make the Land a Free Nation: And yet at this very day, the same people, to whom thou hast made such Protestatins of Liberty, are oppressed by thy Courts, Sizes, Sessions, by thy Justices and Clarks of the Peace, so called, Bayliffs, Committees, are imprisoned, and forced to spend that bread, that should save their lives from Famine.

And all this, Because they stand to maintain an universal Liberty and Freedom, which not only is our Birthright, which our Maker gave us, but which thou hast promised to restore unto us, from under the former oppressing Powers that are gone before, and which likewise we have bought with our Money, in Taxes, Free-quarter, and Bloud-shed; all which Sums thou hast received at our hands, and yet thou hast not given us our bargain.

O thou A-dam, thu Esau, thou Cain, thou Hypocritical man of flesh, when wilt thou cease to kill thy younger Brother? Surely thou must not do this great work of advancing the Creation out of Bondage; for thou art lost extremely, and drowned in the Sea of Covetousnesse, Pride, and hardness of heart. The blessing shall rise out of the dust which thou treadest under foot, Even the poor despised People, and they shall hold up Salvation to this Land, and to all Lands, and thou shalt be ashamed.

Our bodies as yet are in thy hand, our Spirit waits in quiet and peace, upon our Father for Deliverance; and if he give our Bloud into thy hand, for thee to spill, know this, That he is our Almighty Captain: And if some of you will not dare to shed your bloud, to maintain Tyranny and Oppression upon the Creation, know this, That our Bloud and Life shall not be unwilling to be delivered up in meekness to maintain universal Liberty, that so the Curse on our part may be taken off the Creation.

And we shall not do this by force of Arms, we abhorre it, For that is the work of the Midianites, to kill one another; But by obeying the *pacifism — too reliant on Reason.*

Lord of Hosts, who hath Revealed himself in us, and to us, by labouring the Earth in righteousness together, to eate our bread with the sweat of our brows, neither giving hire, nor taking hire, but working together, and eating together, as one man, or as one house of Israel restored from Bondage; and so by the power of Reason, the Law of righteousness in us, we endeavour to lift up the Creation from that bondage of Civil Propriety, which it groans under.

We are made to hold forth this Declaration to you that are the Great Councel, and to you the Great Army of the Land of England, that you may know what we would have, and what you are bound to give us by your Covenants and Promises; and that you may joyn with us in this Work, and so find Peace. Or else, if you do oppose us, we have peace in our Work, and in declaring this Report: And you shall be left without excuse.

The Work we are going about is this, To dig up Georges-Hill and the waste Ground thereabouts, and to Sow Corn, and to eat our bread together by the sweat of our brows.

And the First Reason is this, That we may work in righteousness, and lay the Foundation of making the Earth a Common Treasury for All, both Rich and Poor, That everyone that is born in the land, may be fed by the Earth his Mother that brought him forth, according to the Reason that rules in the Creation. Not Inclosing any part into any particular hand, but all as one man, working together, and feeding together as Sons of one Father, members of one Family; not one Lording over another, but all looking upon each other, as equals in the Creation; so that our Maker may be glorified in the work of his own hands, and that everyone may see, he is no respecter of Persons, but equally loves his whole Creation, and hates nothing but the Serpent, which is Covetousness, branching forth into selvish Imagination, Pride, Envie, Hypocrisie, Uncleanness; all seeking the ease and honor of flesh, and fighting against the Spirit Reason that made the Creation; for that is the Corruption, the Curse, the Devil, the Father of Lies; Death and Bondage that Serpent and Dragon that the Creation is to be delivered from.

And we have moved hereunto for that Reason, and other which hath been shewed us, both by Vision, Voyce, and Revelation.

[Handwritten at top: Freedom Oppression, Murder + Theft are 'materialised' — still idealistic though.]

[Handwritten left margin: dialogues of ... despite abstract dealist categories of ... exploitation]

For it is shewed us, That so long as we, That so long as we, or any other, doth own the Earth to be the peculier Interest of Lords and Landlords, and not common to others as well as them, we own the Curse, and holds the Creation under bondage; and so long as we or any other doth own Landlords and Tennants, for one to call the Land his, or another to hire it of him, or for one to give hire, and for another to work for hire; this is to dishonour the work of Creation; as if the righteous Creator should have respect to persons, and therefore made the Earth for some, and not for all: And so long as we, or any other maintain this Civil Propriety, we consent still to hold the Creation down under that bondage it groans under, and so we should hinder the work of Restoration, and sin against Light that is given into us, and so through fear of the flesh man, lose our peace.

And that this Civil Propriety is the Curse, is manifest thus, Those that Buy and Sell Land, and are landlords, have got it either by Oppression, or Murther, or Theft; and all landlords lives in the breach of the Seventh and Eighth Commandements, Thous shalt not steal, nor kill.

First by their Oppression. They have by their subtle imaginary and covetous wit, got the plain-hearted poor, or yonger Brethren to work for them, for small wages, and by their work have got a great increase; for the poor by their labour lifts up Tyrants to rule over them; or else by their covetous wit, they have out-reached the plain-hearted in Buying and Selling, and thereby inriched themselves, but impoverished others: or else by their subtile wit, having been a lifter up into places of Trust, have inforced people to pay Money for a Publick use, but have divided much of it into their private purses; and so have got it by Oppression.

Then Secondly for Murther; They have by subtile wit and power, pretended to preserve a people in safety by the power of the Sword; and what by large Pay, much Free-quarter, and other Booties, which they call their own, they get much Monies, and with this they buy Land, and become landlords; and if once Landlords, then they rise to be Justices, Rulers, and State Governours, as experience shewes: But all this is but a bloudy and subtile Theevery, countenanced by a Law that Covetousness made; and is a breach of the Seventh Commandement, Thou shalt not kill.

And likewise Thirdly a breach of the Eighth Commandement, Thou shalt not steal; but these landlords have thus stoln the Earth from their fellow Creatures, that have an equal share with them, by the Law of Reason and Creation, as well as they.

And such as these rise up to be rich in the objects of the Earth; then by their plausible words of flattery to the plain-hearted people, whom they deceive, and that lies under confusion and blindness: They are lifted up to be Teachers, Rulers, and Law makers over them that lifted them up; as if the Earth were made peculiarly for them, and not for other weal: If you cast your eye a little backward, you shall see, That this outward Teaching and Ruling power, is the Babylonish yoke laid upon Israel of old, under Nebuchadnezzar; and so Successively from that time, the Conquering Enemy, have still laid these yokes upon Israel to keep Jacob down: And the last enslaving Conquest which the Enemy got over Israel, was the Norman over England; and from that time, Kings, Lords, Judges, Justices, Bayliffs, and the violent bitter people that are Free-holders, are and have been Successively. The Norman Bastard William himself, his Colonels, Captains, inferiour Officers, and Common souldiers, who still are from that time to this day in pursuite of that victory, Imprisoning, Robbing, and killing the poor enslaved English Israelites.

And this appears cleer, For when any Trustee or State Officer is to be Chosen, The Free-holders or Landlords must be the Chusers, who are the Norman Common Souldiers, spread abroad in the Land; And who must be Chosen: but some very rich man, who is the Successor of the Norman Colonels or high Officers. And to what end have they been thus Chosen? but to Establish that Norman power the more forcibly over the enslaved English, and to beat them down again, when as they gather heart to seek for Liberty.

For what are all those Binding and Restraining Laws that have been made from one Age to another since that Conquest, and are still upheld by Furie over the People? I say, What are they? but the Cords, Bands, Manacles, and Yokes that the enslaved English, like Newgate Prisoners, wears upn their hands and legs as they walk the streets; by which those Norman Oppressors, and these their Successors from Age to Age have enslaved the poor People by, killed their younger Brother, and would not suffer Jacob to arise.

O what mighty Delusion, do you, who are the powers of England live in! That while you pretend to throw down that Norman yoke, and Babylonish power, and have promised to make the groaning people of England a Free People; yet you still lift up that Norman yoke, and slavish Tyranny, and holds the People as much in bondage, as the Bastard Conquerour himself, and his Councel of War.

Take notice, That England is not a Free People, till the Poor that have no Land, have a free allowance to dig and labour the Commons, and so live as Comfortably as the Landlords that live in their Inclosures. For the People have not laid out their Monies, and shed their Bloud, that their Landlords, the Norman power, should still have its liberty and freedom to rule in Tyranny in his Lords, landlords, Judges, Justices, Bayliffs, and State Servants; but that the Oppressed might be set Free, Prison doors opened, and the Poor peoples hearts comforted by an universal Consent of making the Earth a Common Treasury, that they may live together as one House of Israel, united in brotherly love into one Spirit; and having a comfortable livelihood in the Community of one Earth their Mother.

If you look through the Earth, you shall see, That the landlords, Teachers and Rulers, are Oppressors, Murtherers, and Theeves in this manner; But it was not thus from the Beginning. And this is one Reason of our digging and labouring the Earth one with another; That we might work in righteousness, and lift up the Creation from bondage: For so long as we own Landlords in this Corrupt Settlement, we cannot work in righteousness; for we should still lift up the Curse, and tread down the Creation, dishonour the Spirit of universal Liberty, and hinder the work of Restauration.

Secondly, In that we begin to Digge upon George-Hill, to eate our Bread together by righteous labour, and sweat of our browes, It was shewed us by Vision in Dreams, and out of Dreams, That that should be the Place we should begin upon; And though that Earth in view of Flesh, be very barren, yet we should trust the Spirit for a blessing. And that not only this Common, or Heath should be taken in and Manured by the People, but all the Commons and waste Ground in England, and in the whole World, shall be taken in by the People in righteousness, not owning any Propriety; but taking the Earth to be a Common Treasury, as it was first made for all.

Thirdly, It is shewed us, That all the Prophecies, Visions, and Revelations of Scriptures, of Prophets, and Apostles, concerning the calling of the Jews, the Restauration of Israel; and making of that People, the Inheritors of the whole Earth; doth all seat themselves in this Work of making the Earth a Common Treasury; as you may read, Ezek. 24.26, 27, &c. Jer. 33.7 to 12. Esay. 49.17, 18, &c. Zach. 8. from 4, to 12, Dan. 2.44, 45, Dan. 7.27. Hos. 14.5, 6,7. Joel 2.26, 27. Amos 9. from 8 to the end, Obad. 17.18.21. Mic. 5. from 7 to the end, Hab. 2.6, 7, 8, 13, 14. Gen. 18.18. Rom. 11.15. Zeph. 3. &c. Zech. 14.9.

And when the Son of man, was gone from the Apostles, his Spirit descended upon the Apostles and Brethren, as they were waiting at Jerusalem; and Rich men sold their Possessions, and gave part to the Poor; and no man said, That ought that he possessed was his own, for they had all things Common, Act. 4.32.

Now this Community was supprest by covetous proud flesh, which was the powers that ruled the world; and the righteous Father suffered himself thus to be suppressed for a time, times and dividing of time, or for 42 months, or for three days and half, which are all but one and the same term of time: And the world is now come to the half day; and the Spirit of Christ, which is the Spirit of universal Community and Freedom is risen, and is rising, and will rise higher and higher, till those pure waters of Shiloe, the Well Springs of Life and Liberty to the whole Creation, do over-run A-dam, and drown those banks of Bondage, Curse and Slavery.

Fourthly, This work to make the Earth a Common Treasury, was shewed us by Voice in Trance, and out of Trance, which which words were these,

Work together, Eate Bread together, Declare this all abroad.

Which Voice was heard Three times: And in Obedience to the Spirit, We have Declared this by Word of mouth, as occasion was offered. Secondly, We have declared it by writing, which others may reade. Thirdly, We have now begun to declare it by Action, in Diging up the Common Land, and casting in Seed that we may eat our Bread together in righteousness. And everyone that comes to work, shall eate the Fruit of their own labours, one having as much Freedom in the Fruit of the Earth as another. Another Voice that was heard was this,

Israel shall neither take Hire, nor give Hire.

And if so, then certainly none shall say, This is my Land, work for me, and IOle give you Wages. For, The Earth is the Lords, that is, Mans, who is Lord of the Creation, in every branch of mankind; perfect; so every particular man is but a member or branch of mankind; and mankind living in the light and obedience to Reason, the King of righteousness, is thereby made a fit and compleat Lord of the Creation. And the whole Earth is this Lords Man, subject to the Spirit. And not the Inheritance of covetous proud Flesh, that is selvish, and enmity to the Spirit.

And if the Earth be not peculiar to any one branch, or branches of manking, but the Inheritance of all; Then is it Free and Common for all, to work together, and eate together.

And truly, you Counsellors and Powers of the Earth, know this, That wheresoever there is a People, thus united by Common Community of livelihood into Oneness, it will become the strongest Land in the World, for then they will be as one man to defend their Inheritance; and Salvation (which is Liberty and Peace) is the Walls and Bulwarks of that Land or City.

Whereas on the otherside, pleading for Propriety and single Interst, divides the People of a land, and the whole world into Parties, and is the cause of all Wars and Bloud-shed, and Contention everywhere.

Another Voice that was heard in a Trance, was this,

Whosoever labours the Earth for any Person or Persons, that are lifted up to rule over others, and doth not look upon themselves, as Equal to others in the Creation: The hand of the Lord shall be upon that Laborer: I the Lord have spoke it, and I will do it.

This Declares likewise to all Laborers, or such as are called Poor people, that they shall not dare to work for Hire, for any Landlord, or for any that is lifted up above others; for by their labours, they have lifted up Tyrants and Tyranny; and by denying to labor for Hire, they shall pull them down again. He that works for another, either for Wages, or to pay him Rent, works unrighteously, and still lifts up the Curse; but they that are resolved to work and eat together, making the Earth a Common Treasury, doth joyn hands with Christ, to lift up the Creation from Bondage, and restores all things from the Curse.

Fiftly, That which does incourage us to go on in this work, is this; we find the streaming out of Love in our hearts towards all; to enemies as well as friends; we would have none live in Beggery, Poverty, or Sorrow, but that everyone might enjoy the benefit of his creation: we have peace in our hearts, and quiet rejoycing in our work, and filled with sweet content, though we have but a dish of roots and bread for our food.

And we are assured, that in the strength of this Spirit that hath manifested himself to us, we shall not be startled, neither at Prison nor Death, while we are about his work; and we have bin made to sit down and count what it may cost us in undertaking such a work, and we know the full sum, and are resolved to give all that we have to buy this Pearl which we see in the Field.

For by this work we are assured, and Reason makes it appear to others, that Bondage shall be removed, Tears wiped away, and all poor People by their righteous Labours shall be relieved, and freed from Poverty and Straits; For is this work of Restoration there will be no begger in Israel: For surely, if there was no Begger in literal Israel, there shall be no Begger in Spiritual Israel the Anti-type, much more.

Sixtly, We have another encouragement that this work shall prosper, Because we see it to be the fulness of Time: For whereas The Son of Man, the Lamb, came in the Fulness of Time, that is, when the Powers of the World made the Earth stink everywhere, by oppressing others, under pretense of worshipping the Spirit rightly, by the Types and Sacrifices of Moses law; the Priests were grown so abominably Covetous and Proud, that they made the People to loathe the Sacrifices and to groan under the Burden of their Oppressing Pride.

Even so now in this Age of the World, that the Spirit is upon his Resurrection, it is likewise the Fulness of Time in a higher measure. For whereas the People generally in former times did rest upon the very observation of the Sacrifices and Types, but persecuted the very name of the Spirit; Even so now, Professors do rest upn the bare observatin of Forms and Customs, and pretend to the Spirit, and yet persecutes, grudges, and hates the power of the Spirit; and as it was then, so it is now: All places stink with the abomination of Self-seeking Teachers and Rulers. For do not I see that everyone Preacheth for money, Counsels for money, and fights for money to maintain particular Interests? And none of these three, that pretend to give liberty to the Creation, do give liberty to the Creation; neither can they, for they are enemies to universal liberty; So that the earth stinks with their Hypocrisie, Covetousness, Envie, sottish Ignorance, and Pride.

The common People are filled with good words from Pulpits and Councel Tables, but no good Deeds; For they wait and wait for good, and for deliverances, but none comes; While they wait for liberty, behold greater bondage comes insteed of it, and burdens, oppressions, taskmasters, from Sessions, Lawyers, Bayliffs of Hundreds, Committees, Impropriators, Clerks of Peace, and Courts of Justice, so called, does whip the People by old Popish weather-beaten Laws, that were excommunicate long age by Covenants, Oaths, and Ordinances; but as yet are not cast out, but rather taken in again, to be standing pricks in our eys, and thorns in our side; Beside Free-quartering, Plundering by some rude Souldiers, and the abounding of Taxes; which if they were equally divided among the Souldiery, and not too much bagd up in the hands of particulars Officers and Trustees, there would be less complaining: Besides the horrible cheating that is in Buying and Selling, and the cruel Oppression of Landlords, and Lords of Mannours, and quarter Sessions; Many that have bin good Souldiers, and so to fight to uphold the Curse, or else live in great straits and beggery: O you A-dams of the Earth, you have right Clothing, full Bellies, have your Honors and Ease, and you puffe at this; But know thous stout-hearted Pharoah, that the day of Judgement is begun, and it will reach to thee ere long; Jacob hath bin very low, but he is rising, and will rise, do the worst thou canst; and the poor people whom thou oppresses, shall be the Saviours of the land; For the blessing is rising up in them, and thou shalt be ashamed.

And thus, you Powers of England, and of the whole World, we have declared our Reasons, why we have begun to dug upon George hill in Surrey. One thing I must tell you more, in the close, which I received in voce likewise at another time; and when I received it, my eye was set towards you. The words were these:

Let Israel go free.

Surely, as Israel lay 430 years under Pharoahs' bondage, before Moses was sent to fetch them out: even so Israel (the Elect Spirit spread in Sons and Daughters) hath lain three times so long already, which is the Anti-type, under your Bondage, and cruel Taskmasters: But now the time of Deliverance is come, and thou proud Esau, and stout-hearted Covetousness, thou must come down, and be lord of the Creation no longer. For now the King of Righteousness is rising to Rule In, and Over the Earth.

Therefore, if thou wilt find Mercy, Let Israel go Free; break in pieces quickly the Band of particular Propriety, dis-own this oppressing Murder, Oppressin and Thievery of Buying and Selling of Land, owning of landlords, and paying of Rents, and give thy Free Consent to make the Earth a Common Treasury, without grumbling; That the younger Brethren may live comfortably upon Earth, as well as the Elder: That all may enjoy the benefit of their Creation.

And hereby thou wilt Honour thy Father, and thy Mother. Thy Father, which is the Spirit of Community, that made all, and that dwels in all. Thy Mother, which is the Earth, that brought us all forth: That as a true Mother, loves all her Children. Therefore do not thou hinder the Mother Earth, from giving all her Children such, by thy Inclosing it into particular hands, and holding up that cursed Bondage of Inclosure by thy Power.

And then thou wilt repent of thy Theft, in maintaining the breach of the eight Commandment, by Stealing the Land as I say from thy fellow-creatures, or younger Brothers: which thou and all thy landlords have, and do live in the breach of that Commandment.

Then thou wilt Own no other God, or Ruling Power, but One, which is the King of Righteousness, ruling and dwelling in everyone, and in the whole; whereas now thou hast many gods: For Covetousness is thy God, Pride, and an Envious murdering Humor (to kill one by Prison or Gallows, that crosses thee, though their cause be pure, sound, and good reason) is thy God, Self-love, and slavish Fear (lest others serve thee as thou hast served them) is thy god, Hypocrisie, Fleshly Imagination, that keeps no Promise, Covenant, nor Protestation, is thy God: love of Money, Honor, and Ease, is thy God: And all these, and the like Ruling Powers, makes thee Blind, and hard-hearted, that thou does not, nor cannot lay to heart the affliction of others, though they dy for want of bread, in that rich City, undone under your eys.

Therefore once more, Let Israel go Free, that the poor may labour the Waste land, and such the Brests of their mother Earth, that they starve not: And in so doing, thou wilt keep the Sabbath day, which is a day of Rest; sweetly enjoying the Peace of the Spirit of Righteousness; and find Peace, by living among a people that live in peace; this will be a day of Rest which thou never knew yet.

But I do not entreat thee, for thous art not to be intreated, but in the Name of the lord, that hath drawn me forth to speak to thee; I, yea I say, I Command thee, to let Israel go Free, and quietly to gather together into the place where I shall appoint; and hold them no longer in bondage.

And thou A-dam that holds the Earth in slavery under the Curse: If thou wilt not let Israel go Free; for thou being the Antitype, will be more stout and lusty then the Egyptian Paroah of old, who was thy Type; Then know, That whereas I brought Ten Plagues upon him, I will Multiply may Plagues upon thee, till I make thee weary, and miserably ashamed: And I will bring out my People with a strong hand, and stretched out arme.

Thus we have discharged our Souls in declaring the Cause of our Digging upon George-Hill in Surrey, that the Great Councel and Army of the Land may take notice of it, That there is no intent of Tumult or Fighting, but only to get Bread to eat, with the sweat of our brows; working together in righteousness, and eating the blessings of the Earth in peace.

And if any of you that are the great Ones of the Earth, that have been bred tenderly, and cannot word, do bring in your Stock into this Commond Treasury as an Offering to the work of Righteousness; we will work for you, and you shall receive as we receive. But if you will not, but Paroah like cry, Who is the Lord that we should obey him?

and endeavour to Oppose, then know, That he that delivered Israel from Pharoah of old, is the same Power still, in whom we trust, and whom we serve; for this Conquest over thee shall be got, not by Sword or Weapon, but by my Spirit saith the Lord of Hosts.

[handwritten: That's unfortunate]

A Declaration from the Poor Oppressed People of England

We whose narnes are subscribed, do in the name of all the poor oppressed people in *England*, declare unto you, that call your selves lords of Manors, and Lords of the Land, That in regard the King of Righteousness, our Maker, hath inlightened our hearts so far, as to see, That the earth was not made purposely for you, to be Lords of it, and we to be your Slaves, Servants, and Beggers; but it was made to be a common Livelihood to all, without respect of persons: And that your buying and selling of Land, and the Fruits of it, one to another, is *The cursed thing*, and was brought in by War; which hath, and still does establish murder, and theft, In the hands of some branches of Mankinde over others, which is the greatest outward burden, and unrighteous power, that the Creation groans under: For the power of inclosing Land, and owning Propriety, was brought into the Creation by your Ancestors by the Sword; which first did murther their fellow Creatures, Men, and after plunder or steal away their Land, and left this Land successively to you, their Children. And therefore, though you did not kill or theeve, yet you hold that cursed thing in your hand, by the power of the Sword; and so you justifie the wicked deeds of your Fathers; and that sin of your Fathers, shall be visited upon the Head of you, and your Children, to the third and fourth generation, and longer too, till your bloody and theeving power be rooted out of the Land.

And further, in regard the King of Righteousness hath made us sensible of our burthens, and the cryes and groanings of our hearts are come before him: We take it as a testimony of love from him, That our hearts begin to be freed from slavish fear of men, such as you are; and that we find Resolutions in us, grounded upon the inward law of Love, one towards another, To Dig and Plough up the Commons, and waste Lands through *England;* and that our conversation shall be so unblameable, That your Laws shall not reach to oppress us any longer, unless you by your Laws will shed the innocent blood that runs in our veins.

For though you and your Ancestors got your Propriety by murther and theft, and you keep it by the same power from us, that have an equal right to the Land with you, by the righteous Law of Creation, yet we shall have no occasion of quarrelling (as you do) about that disturbing devil, called *Particular propriety*: For the Earth, with all her Fruits of Corn, Cattle, and such like, was made to be a common Store-house of Livelihood to all Mankinde, friend, and foe, without exception.

And to prevent your scrupulous Objections, know this, That we Must neither buy nor sell; Money must not any longer (after our work of the Earths community is advanced) be the great god, that hedges in some, and hedges out others; for Money is but part of the Earth: And surely, the Righteous Creator, who is King, did never ordain, That unless some of Mankinde, do bring that Mineral (silver and gold) in their hands, to others of their own kinde, that they should neither be fed, nor be clothed; no surely, For this was the project of Tyrant-flesh (which Land-lords are branches of) to set his Image upon Money. And they make this unrighteous Law, That none should buy or sell, eat, or be clothed, or have any comfortable Livelihood among men, unless they did bring his Image stamped upon Gold or Silver in their hands.

And whereas the Scriptures speak, That the mark of the Beast is 666, the number of a man; and that those that do not bring that mark in their hands, or in their foreheads, they should neither buy nor sell, *Revel*. 13.16. And seeing the numbering Letters round about the English money make 666, which is the number of that Kingly Power and Glory, (called a *Man*) And seeing the age of the Creation is now come to the Image of the Beast, or Half day. And seeing 666 is his mark, we expect this to be the last Tyrannical power that shall raign; and that people shall live freely in the enioyment of the Earth, without bringing the mark of the Beast in their hands, or in their promise; and that they shall buy Wine and Milk, without money, or without price, as *Isiah* speaks.

For after our work of the Earthly community is advanced, we must make use of Gold and Silver, as we do of other metals, but not to buy and sell withal; for buying and selling is the great cheat, that robs and steals the Earth one from another: It is that which makes some Lords, others Beggers, some Rulers, others to be ruled; and makes great Murderers and Theeves to be imprisoners, and hangers of little ones, or of sincere-hearted men.

And while we are made to labor the Earth together, with one consent and willing minde; and while we are made free, that everyone, friend and foe, shall enjoy the benefit of their Creation, that is, To have food and rayment from the Earth, their Mother; and everyone subiect to give accompt of his thoughts, words, and actions to none, but to the one onely righteous Judg, and Prince of Peace; the Spirit of Righteousness that dwells, and that is now rising up to rule in every Creature, and in the whole Globe. We say, while we are made to hinder no man of his Priviledges given him in his Creation, equal to one, as to another; what Law then can you make, to take hold upon us, but Laws of Oppression and Tyranny, that shall enslave or spill the blood of the Innocent? And so your Selves, your Judges, Lawyers, and Justices, shall be found to be the greatest Transgressors, in, and over Mankinde.

But to draw neerer to declare our meaning, what we would have, and what we shall endevor to the uttermost to obtain, as moderate and righteous Reason directs us; seeing we are made to see our Privileages, given us in our Creation, which have hitherto been denied to us, and our Fathers, since the power of the Sword began to rule, And the secrets of the Creation have been locked up under the traditional, Parrat-like speaking, from the Universities, and Colledges for Scolars, And since the power of the murdering, and theeving Sword, formerly, as well as now of late yeers, hath set up a Govenment, and maintains that Government; for what are prisons, and putting others to death, but the power of the Sword to enforce people to that Government which was got by Conquest and Sword, and cannot stand of it self, but by the same murdering power? That Government that is got over people by the Sword and kept by the Sword, is not set up by the King of Righteousness to be his Law, but by Covetousness, the great god of the world; who hath been permitted to raign for a time, times, and dividing of time and his government draws to the period of the last term of his allotted time; and then the Nations shall see the glory of that Government that shall rule in Righteousness, without either Sword or Spear,

And seeing further, the power of Righteousness in our hearts, seeking the livelihood of others as well as our selves, hath drawn forth our bodies to begin to dig, and plough, in the Commons and waste Land, for the reasons already declared,

And seeing and finding ourselves poor, wanting Food to feed upon, while we labor the Earth to cast in seed, and to wait till the first crop comes up; and wanting Ploughs, Carts, Corn, and such materials to plant the Commons withal, we are willing to declare our condition to you, and to all, that have the Treasury of the Earth, locked up in your Bags, Chests, and Barns, and will offer up nothing to this publike Treasury; but will rather see your fellow Creatures starve for want of Bread, that have an equal right to it with your selves, by the Law of Creation: But this by the way we onely declare to you, and to all that follow the subtle art of buying and selling the Earth with her Fruits, meerly to get the Treasury thereof into their hands, to lock it up from them, to whom it belongs; that so, such covetous, proud, unrighteous, selfish flesh, may be left without excuse in the day of Judgment.

And therefore, the main thing we aym at, and for which we declare our Resolutions to go forth, and act, is this, To lay hold upon, and as we stand in need, to cut and fell, and make the best advantage we can of the Woods and Trees, that grow upon the Commons, To be a stock for our selves, and our poor Brethren, through the land of *England*, to plant the Commons withal; and to provide us bread to eat, till the Fruit of our labors in the Earth bring forth increase; and we shall meddle with none of your Proprieties (but what is called Commonage) till the Spirit in you, make you cast up your Lands and Goods, which were got, and still is kept in your hands by murder, and theft; and then we shall take it from the Spirit, that hath conquered you, and not from our Swords, which is an abominable, and unrighteous power, and a destroyer of the Creation: But the Son of man comes not to destroy, but to save.

And we are moved to send forth this Declaration abroad, to give notice to everyone whom it concerns, in regard we hear and see, that some of you, that have been Lords of Manors, do cause the Trees and Woods that grow upon the Commons, which you pretend a Royalty unto, to be cut down and sold, for your own private use, Thereby the Common Land, which your own mouths doe say belongs to the poor, is impoverished, and the poor oppressed people robbed of their Rights, while you give them cheating words, by telling some of our poor oppressed Brethren, That those of us that have begun to Dig and Plough up the Commons, will hinder the poor; and so blinde their eyes, that they see not their Priviledge, while you, and the rich Free-holders make the most profit of the Commons, by your over-stocking of them with Sheep and Cattle; and the poor that have the name to own the Commons, have the least share therein; nay, they are checked by you, if they cut Wood, Heath, Turf, or Furseys, in places about the Common, where you disallow.

Therefore we are resolved to be cheated no longer, nor be held under the slavish fear of you no longer, seing the Earth was made for us, as well as for you. And if the Common Land belongs to us who are the poor oppressed, surely the woods that grow upon the Commons belong to us likewise: therefore we are resolved to try the uttermost in the light of reason, to know whether we shall be free men, or slaves. If we lie still, and let you steale away our Birthrights, we perish; and if we Petition we perish also, though we have paid taxes, given free quarter, and ventured our lives to preserve the Nations freedom as much as you, and therefore by the law of contract with you, freedom in the land is our portion as well as yours, equal with you: And if we strive for freedom, and your murdering, governing Laws destroy us, we can but perish.

Therefore we require, and we resolve to take both Common Land, and Common woods to be a livelihood for us, and look upon you as equal with us, not above us, knowing very well, that *England* the land of our Nativity, is to be a common Treasury of livelihood to all, without respect of persons.

So then, we declare unto you, that do intend to cut our Common Woods and Trees, that you shall not do it; unlesse it be for a stock for us, as aforesaid, and we to know of it, by a publick declaration abroad, that the poor oppressed, that live thereabouts, may take it, and employ it, for their publike use, therefore take notice we have demanded it in the name of the Commons of *England*, and of all the Nations of the world, it being the righteous freedom of the Creation.

Likewise we declare to you that have begun to cut down our Common Woods and Trees, and to fell and carry away the same for your private use, that you shall forbear, and go no farther, hoping, that none that are friends to the Commonwealth of England, will endeavour to buy any of those Common Trees and Woods of any of those Lords of Mannors, so called, who have, by the murdering and cheating law of the sword, stoln the Land from younger brothers, who have by the law of Creation, a standing portion in the Land, as well, and equall with others. Therefore we hope all Wood-mongers will disown all such private merchandise, as being a robbing of the poor oppressed, and take notice, that they have been told our resolution: But if any of you that are Wood-mongers, will buy it of the poor, and for their use, to stock the Commons, from such as may be appointed by us to sell it, you shall have it quietly, without diminution; but if you will slight us in this thing, blame us not, if we make stop of the Carts you send and convert the Woods to our own use, as need requires, it being our own, equal with him that calls himself the Lord of the Mannor, and not his peculiar right, shutting us out, but he shall share with us as a fellow-creature.

For we say our purpose is, to take those Common Woods to sell them, now at first, to be a stock for our selves, and our children after us, to plant and manure the Common land withall; for we shall endeavour by our righteous acting not to leave the earth any longer intangled unto our children, by self-seeking proprietors; But to leave it a free store-house, and common treasury to all, without respect of persons; And this we count is our dutie, to endeavour to the uttermost, every man in his place (according to the nationall Covenant which the Parliament set forth) a Reformation to preserve the peoples liberties, one as well as another: As well those as have paid taxes, and given free quarter, as those that have either born the sword, or taken our moneys to dispose of them for publike use: for if the Reformation must be according to the word of God, then everyone is to have the benefit and freedom of his creation, without respect of persons; we count this our duty, we say, to endeavour to the uttermost, and so shall leave those that rise up to oppose us without excuse, in their day of Judgment; and our precious blood, we hope, shall not be dear to us, to be willingly laid down at the door of a prison, or foot of a gallows, to justifie this righteous cause; if those that have taken our money from us, and promised to give us freedom for it, should turn Tyrants against us: for we must not fight, but suffer.

And further we intend, that not one, two, or a few men of us shall sell or exchange the said woods, but it shall be known publikly in Print or writing to all, how much every such, and such parcell of wood is sold for, and how it is laid out, either in victualls, corn, ploughs, or other materials necessary.

And we hope we may not doubt (at least we expect) that they that are called the great Councel and powers of *England*, who so often have declared themselves, by promises and Covenants, and confirmed them by multitude of fasting daies, and devout Protestations, to make *England* a free people, upon condition they would pay moneys, and adventure their lives against the successor of the *Norman* Conqueror; under whose oppressing power *England* was enslaved; And we look upon that freedom promised to be the inheritance of all, without respect of persons; And this cannot be, unless the Land of *England* be freely set at liberty from proprietors, and become a common Treasury to all her children, as every portion of the Land of *Canaan* was the Common livelihood of such and such a Tribe, and of every member in that Tribe, without exception, neither hedging in any, nor hedging out.

We say we hope we need not doubt of their sincerity to us herein, and that they will not gainsay our determinate course; howsoever, their actions will prove to the view of all, either their sinceritie, or hypocrisie: We know what we speak is our priviledge, and our cause is righteous, and if they doubt of it, let them but send a childe for us to come before them, and we shall make it manifest four wayes.

First, by the National Covenant, which yet stands in force to bind Parliament and people to be faithful and sincere, before the Lord God Almighty, wherein everyone in his several place hath covenanted to preserve and seek the liberty each of other, without respect of persons.

Secondly, by the late Victory over King *Charls*, we do claime this our pnviledge, to be quietly given us, out of the hands of Tyrant-Government, as our bargain and contract with them; for the Parliament promised, if we would pay taxes, and give free quarter, and adventure our lives against *Charls* and his party, whom they called the Common enemy, they would make us a free people; These three being all done by us, as well as by themselves, we claim this our bargain, by the law of contract from them, to be a free people with them, and to have an equall priviledge of Common livelihood with them, they being chosen by us, but for a peculiar worke, and for an appointed time, from among us, not to be our oppressing Lords, but servants to succour us. But these two are our weakest proofs. And yet by them (in the light of reason and equity that dwells in mens hearts) we shall with ease cast down, all those former enslaving *Norman* reiterated laws, in every Kings raigne since the Conquest, which are as thornes in our eyes, and pricks in our sides, and which are called the Ancient Government of *England*.

Thirdly we shall prove that we have a free right to the land of *England*, being born therein as well as elder brothers, and that it is our equal right with them, and they with us, to have a comfortable livlihood in the earth, without owning any of our own kinde, to be either Lords, or Land-Lords over us: And this we shall prove by plain Text of Scripture, without exposition upon them, which the Scholars and great ones generally say, is their rule to walk by.

Fourthly, we shall prove it by the Righteous Law of our Creation, That mankinde in all his branches, is the Lord of the Earth and ought not to be in subjection to any of his own kinde without him, but to live in the light of the law of righteousness, and peace established in his heart.

And thus in love we have declared the purpose of our hearts plainly, without flatterie, expecting love, and the same sincerity from you, without grumbling or quarreling, being Creatures of your own Image and mould, intending no other matter herein, but to observe the Law of righteous action, endeavouring to shut out of the Creation, the cursed thing, called *Particular Propriety*, which is the cause of all wars, bloud-shed, theft, and enslaving Laws, that hold the people under miserie.

Signed for and in behalf of all the poor oppressed people of *England*, and the whole world.

Gerrard Winstanley, John Coulton, John Palmer, Thomas Star, Samuel Webb, John Hayman, Thomas Edcer, William Hogrill, Daniel Weeden, Richard

Wheeler, Nathaniel Yates, William Clifford, John Harrison, Thomas Hayden, James Hall, James Manley, Thomas Barnard, John South, Robert Sayer, Christopher Clifford, John Beechee, William Coomes, Christopher Boncher, Richard Taylor, Urian Worthington, Nathaniel Holcombe, Giles Childe, senior *John Webb, Thomas Yarwel, William Bonnington, John Ash, Ralph Ayer, John Pra, John Wilkinson, Anthony Spire, Thomas East, Allen Brown, Edward Parret, Richard Gray, John Mordy, John Bachilor, William Childe, William Hatham, Edward Wicher, William Tench.*

A New-Year's Gift for the Parliament and Army:

SHEWING, WHAT THE KINGLY POWER IS; AND THAT THE CAUSE OF THOSE THEY CALL DIGGERS IS THE LIFE AND MARROW OF THAT CAUSE THE PARLIAMENT HATH DECLARED FOR, AND THE ARMY FOUGHT FOR; THE PERFECTING OF WHICH WORK, WILL PROVE *ENGLAND* TO BE THE FIRST OF NATIONS, OR THE TENTH PART OF THE CITY *BABYLON*, THAT FALLS OFF FROM THE BEAST FIRST, AND THAT SETS THE CROWN UPON CHRISTS HEAD, TO GOVERN THE WORLD IN RIGHTEOUSNESS:

> *Die Pride and Envie; Flesh, take the poor's advice.*
> *Covetousnesse be gon: Come, Truth and Love arise.*
> *Patience take the Crown; throw Anger out of dores:*
> *Cast out Hypocrisie and Lust, which follows whores:*
> *Then* England *sit in rest; Thy sorrows will have end;*
> *Thy Sons will live in peace, and each will be a friend.*

Gentlemen of the Parliament and Armie; you and the Common people have asssted each other, to cast out the Head of oppression which was Kingly power, seated in one mans hand, and that work is now done, and till that work was done you called upon the people to assist you to deliver this distressed bleeding dying nation out of bondage; And the people came and failed you not, counting neither purse nor blood too dear to part with to effect this work.

The Parliament after this have made an Act to cast out Kingly power, and to make *England* a free Common-wealth. These Acts the People are much rejoyced with, as being words forerunning their freedome, and they wait for their accomplishment that their joy may be full; for as words without action are a cheat, and kills the comfort of a righteous spirit, so words performed in action does comfort and nourish the life thereof.

Now Sirs, wheresoever we spie out Kingly power, no man I hope shall be troubled to declare it, nor afraid to cast it out, having both Act of Parliament, the Souldiers Oath, and the common peoples consent on his side; for Kingly power is like a great spread tree, if you lop the head or top-bow, and let the other Branches and root stand, it will grow again and recover fresher strength.

If any ask me, What Kingly power is? I Answer, there is a twofold Kingly power. The one is, the Kingly power of righteousnesse, and this is the power of Almightie God, ruling the whole creation in peace, and keeping it together. And this is the power of universal love, leading people into all truth, teaching everyone to doe as he would be done unto. Now once more striving with flesh and blood, shaking down every thing that cannot stand, and bringing everyone into the Unitie of himself, the one Spirit of love and righteousnesse, and so will work a through restauration. But this Kingly power is above all, and will tread-all covetousness, pride, envy, and self-love, and all other enemies whatsoever, under his feet and take the kingdom and government of the Creation out of the hand of self-seeking and self-honouring Flesh, and rule the alone King of Righteousness in the earth; and this indeed is Christ himself, who will cast out the curse; But this is not that Kingly power intended by that Act of Parliament to be cast out, but pretended to be set up, though this Kingly power be much fought against both by Parliament, Armie, Clergy, and people; but when the are made to see him, then they shall mourn, because they have persecuted him.

But the other Kingly power, is the power of unrighteousness, which indeed is the Devil; And O that there were such a heart in Parliament and Army, as to perform your own Act; then People would never complain of you for breach of Covenant, for your Covetousness, Pride, and too much Self-seeking that is in you. And you on the other-side would never have cause to complain of the Peoples murmurings against you. Truly this jarring that is between you and the People is, The Kingly power; yea that very Kingly power which you have made an Act to cast out; therefore see it be fulfilled on your part; for the Kingly power of Righteousness expects it, or else he will cast you out for Hypocrites and unsavory Salt; for he looks upon all your Actions, and truly there is abundance of Rust about your Actings, which makes them that they do not shine bright.

This Kingly power, is covetousness in his branches, or the power of self-love, ruling in one or in many men over others, and enslaving those who in the Creation are their equals; nay, who are in the strictness of equity rather their Masters: And this Kingly power is usually set in the Chair of Government, under the name of Prerogative, when he rules in one, over other: And under the name of State Priviledge of Parliament, when he rules in many over others: and this Kingly power, is alwayes raised up, and established by the Sword, and therefore he is called the Murderer, or the great red Dragon, which fights against *Michael*, for he enslaves the weakness of the People under him, denying an equal freedom in the Earth to everyone, which the Law of Righteousness gave every man in his creation. This I say is Kingly power under darkness, and as he rules in men, so he makes men jar one against another, and is the cause of all Wars and Complainings; he is known by his outward actions, and his action at this very day fills all places; for this power of darkness rules, and would rule, and is that only Enemy that fights against Creation and National Freedom: And this Kingly power is he, which you have made an Act of Parliament to cast out. And now you Rulers of *England*, play the men, and be valiant for the Truth, which is Christ: for assure your selves God will not be mocked, nor the Devil will not be mocked; for First you say and profess you own the Scriptures of Prophets and Apostles, and God looks that you should perform that Word in action: Secondly you have Declared against the Devil, and if you do not now go through with your work, but slack your hand by hypocritical self-love, and so suffer this dark Kingly power to rise higher and Rule, you shall find, he will maule both you, and yours to purpose.

The life of this dark Kingly power, which you have made an Act of Parliament and Oath to cast out, if you search it to the bottom, you shall see it lies within the iron chest of cursed Covetousness, Who gives the Earth to some part of mankind, and denies it to another part of mankind: and that part that hath the Earth, hath no right from the Law of creation to take it to himself, and shut out others; but he took it away violently by Theft and Murder in Conquest: As when our Norman *William* came into *England* and conquered, he turned the English out, and gave the Land unto his Norman Souldiers every man his parcel to inclose, and hence rose up Propriety; for this is the fruit if War from the beginning, for it removes Propriety out of a weaker into a stronger hand, but still upholds the curse of Bondage; and hereby the Kingly power which you have made an Act, and Sworn to cast out, does remove himself from one chair to another; and so long as the Sword rules over brethren, (mind what I say) so long the Kingly power of darkness Rules, and so large as yet is his Kingdom; which spreads from Sea to Sea, and fills the Earth; but Christ is rising who will take the Dominion and Kingdom out of his hand, and his power of Righteousness, shall rise and spred from East to West, from North to South, and fill the Earth with himself, and cast the other cursed power out, when Covetousness sheaths his Sword, and ceases to rage in the field; he first makes sharp Laws of Bondage, That those that are conquered, and that by him are appointed not to enjoy the Earth, but are turned out, shall be Servants, Slaves, and Vassals to the Conquerers party: so those Laws that upholds Whips, Prisons, Gallows is but the same power of the Sword that raged, and that was drunk with Blood in the field.

King *Charles*, it is true, was the Head of this Kingly power in *England*, and he Reigned as he was a Successor of the last Norman Conquerer: and whosoever you be, that hath Propriety of Land, hath your Titles and Evidences made to you in his or his Ancestors Name, and from his and their Will and Kingly Power; I am sure, he was not our Creator, and therefore parcelled out the Earth to some, and denied it to others, therefore he must needs stand as a Conquerer, and was the Head of this Kingly power, that burden and oppresses the People, and that is the cause of all our Wars and Divisions; for if this Kingly power of Covetousness, which is the unrighteous Divider, did not yet Rule: both Parliament, Army, and rich People ', would cheerfully give consent that those we call Poor should Dig and freely plant the Waste and Common Land for a livelihood, seeing there is Land enough, and more by half then is made use of, and not be suffered to perish for want. And yet O ye Rulers of *England*, you make a blazing profession,

That you know, and that you own God, Christ, and the Scriptures: but did Christ ever declare such hardness of heart? did not he bid the rich man go and sell all that he hath and give to the Poor? and does not the Scripture say, If thou makest a Covenant, keep it, though it be to thy loss: But truly it will not be to your loss, to let your fellow Creatures, your equals in the Creation, nay those that have been faithful in your Cause, and so your Friends; I say it will not be to your loss to let them quietly improve the Waste and Common Land, that they may live in peace, freed from the heavie burdens of Poverty; for hereby our own Land will be increased with all sorts of Commodities, and the People will be knit together in love, to keep out a forreign Enemy that endeavours, and that will endeavour as yet, to come like an Army of cursed Ratts and Mice to destroy our inheritance; so that if this Freedom be quietly granted to us, you grant it but to your selves, to English-men, to your own flesh and blood: and you do but give us our own neither, which Covetousness, in the Kingly power hath, and yet does hold from us; for the Earth in the first Creation of it, was freely given to whole mankind, without respect of Persons; therefore you Lords of Mannors, and you Rulers of *England*, if you own God, Christ and Scripture, now make Restitution, and deliver us quiet possession of our Land, which the Kingly power as yet holds from us.

While this Kingly power raigned in one man called *Charls*, all sort of people complained of oppression, both Gentrie and Common people, because their lands, inclosures, and Copie-holds were intangled, and because their Trades were destroyed by Monopolizing Patentees, and your troubles were that you could not live free from oppression in the earth: Thereupon you that were the Gentrie when you were assembled in Parliament, you called upon the poor Common People to come and help you, and cast out oppression and you that complained are helped and freed, and that top-bow is lopped off the tree of Tyrannie, and Kingly power in that one particular is cast out; but alas oppression is a great tree still, and keeps off the son of freedome from the poor Commons still, he hath many branches and great roots which must be grub'd up, before everyone can sing Sions songs in peace.

As we spie out Kingly power we must declare it, and cast it out, or else we shall deny the Parliament of *England* and their Acts, and so prove Traitors to the Land, by denying obedience thereunto. Now there are Three Branches more of Kinglie power greater then the former that oppresses this Land wonderfully; and these are the power of the Tithing Priests over the Tenths of our labours; and the power of Lords of Mannors, holding the free use of the Commons, and wast Land from the poor, and the intolerable oppression either of bad Laws, or of bad Judges corrupting good Laws; these are branches of the Norman conquest and Kingly power still, and wants a Reformation.

For as the first, *William* the Conqueror promised, That if the Clergie would preach him up, so that the people might be bewitched, so as to receive him to be Gods Anointed over them, he would give them the Tenths of the Lands increase yeerly; and they did it, and he made good his Promise; and do we not yet see, That if the Clergie can get tithes or Money, they will turn as the Ruling power turns, any way; to Popery, to Protestantisme; for a King, against a King, for Monarchy, for State-Government; they cry who bids most wages, they will be on the strongest side, for an Earthly maintenance; yea, and when they are lifted up, they woud Rule too, because they are called Spiritual men: It is true indeed, they are spiritual; but it is of the spiritual power of Covetousness and Pride; for the spiritual power of Love and Righteousness they know not; for if they knew it, they would not persecute and raile against him as they do. The Clergie will serve on any side, like our ancient Laws, that will serve any master: They will serve the Papists, they will serve the Protestants, they will serve the King, they will serve the States; they are one and the same Tools for Lawyers to work with under any Government. O you Parliament-men of *England,* cast those whorish Laws out of doors, that are so Common, that pretend love to everyone, and is faithful to none; for truly, he that goes to Law, as the Proverb is, shall die a Beggar: so that old Whores, and old Laws, picks mens pockets, and undoes them: If the fault lie in the Laws, and much does, burn all your old Law-Books in *Cheapside,* & set up a Government upon your own Foundation: do not put new Wine into old Bottles; but as your Government must be new, so let the Laws be new, or else you will run farther into the Mud, where you stick already, as though you were fast in an*Irish* Bogge; for you are so far sunke, that he must have good eyes that can see where you are: but yet all are not blind, there are eyes that sees you: but if the fault lies in the Judges of the Law, surely such men deserve no power in a Reforming Common-wealth, that burdens all sorts of People.

And truly Ile tell you plain, your Two Acts of Parliament are excellent and Righteous: The One to cast out Kingly power; The Other to make *England* a Free Common-wealth: build upon these Two, it is a firm Foundation, and your House will be the glory of the World; and I am confident, the righteous Spirit will love you: do not stick in the Bogge of Covetousness; Let not self-love so be-muddy your brain, that you should lose your selves in the thicket of bramble bush-words, and set never a strong Oak of some stable Action for the Freedome of the poor Oppressed that helped you when you complained of Oppression. Let not Pride blind your eyes, that you should forget you are the Nations Servants, and so prove *Solomons* words good in your selves, That Servants ride on Horse-back and Coaches, when as Princes, such as Chose you, and set you there, go on foot: and many of them, through their love to the Nation, have so wasted themselves, that now they can hardly get Bread, but with great difficulty. I tell you this is a sore Evil, and this is truth; therefore think upon it, it is a poor mans Advice, and you shall finde weight in it, if you Do as well as Say.

Then Secondly for Lords of Mannors, They were *William* the Conquerors Colonels and Favourites, and he gave a large circuit of Land to everyone, called A Lord-ship, that they might have a watchful eye, that if any of the conquered English should begin to Plant themselves upon any Common or waste Land, to live out of sight or out of slavery, that then some Lord of Mannour or other might see and know of it, and drive them off, as these Lords of Mannors now a dayes, endeavours to drive off the Diggers from Digging upon the Commons; but we expect the Rulers of the Land will grant unto us their Friends, the benefit of their own Acts against Kingly power, and not suffer that Norman power to crush the poor Oppressed, who helped them in their straits, nor suffer that Norman power to bud fresher out, & so in time may come to over-top our deer bought Freedom more then ever.

Search all your Laws, and Ile adventure my life, for I have little else to lose, That all Lords of Mannors hold Title to the Commons by no stronger hold then the Kings Will, whose Head is cut off; and the King held Title as he was a Conqueror; now if you cast off the King who was the Head of that power, surely the power of Lords of Mannors is the same; therefore performe your own Act of Parliament, and cast out that part of the Kinglie power likewise, that the People may see you understand what you Say and Do, and that you are faithfull.

For truly the Kinglie power reigns strongly in the Lords of Mannors over the Poor; for my own particular, I have in other Writings as well as in this, Declared my Reasons, That the common Land is the poor Peoples Proprietie; and I have Digged upon the Commons, and I hope in time to obtain the Freedom, to get Food and Raiment therefrom by righteous labour, which is all I desire; and for so doing, the supposed Lord of that Mannor hath Arrested me twice; First, in an Action of £20. Trespass for Plowing upon the Commons, which I never did; and because they would not suffer me to Plead my own Cause, they made shift to pass a Sentence of Execution against some Cows I kept, supposing they had been mine, and took them away; but the right owner reprieved them, & fetched the Cowes back; so greedy are these Theeves and Murderers after my life for speaking the truth, and for maintaining the Life and Marrow of the Parliaments cause in my Actions.

And now they have Arrested me again in an Action of £4. trespas for digging upon the Comons, which I did, & own the work to be righteous & no trespas to any: This was the Attorney of *Kingstone's* Advice, either to get Money on both sides, for they love Mony as deerly as a poor mans dog do his breakfast in a cold morning (but regard not justice) or else, That I should not remove it to a higher Court, but that the cause might be tryed there, and then they know how to please the Lords of Mannors, that have resolved to spend hundreds of pounds but they will hinder the poor from enjoying the Commons; for they will not suffer me to plead my own Cause, but I must not Fee an enemie, or else be condemned and executed without mercy or Justice as I was before, and so to put me in Prison till I pay their unrighteous Sentence; for truly Attourneys are such neat workmen, that they can turn a Cause which way those that have the biggest purse will have them: and the Countrie knows very well, That *Kingstone* court is so full of the Kinglie power; that some will rather lose their Rights, then have their causes tryed there: one of the Officers of that court, told a friend of mine, That if the Diggers cause was good, he would pick out such a jurie as should overthrow him: And upon my former Arrest, they picked out such a jurie as Sentenced me to pay £10. damages for Plowing upon the commons, which I did not do, neither did any witness prove it before them: So that from *Kingstone* Juries, Lords of Mannors, and Kinglie power, *Good Lord deliver us.*

Do these men obey the Parliaments Acts, to throw down Kinglie power? O no: The same unrighteous doing that was complained of in King *Charls* dayes, the same doings is among them still: Monies will buy and sell Justice still: and is our 8 yeers Wars come round about to lay us down again in the kennel of injustice as much or more then before? are we no farther learned yet? O ye Rulers of *England,* when must we turn over a new leaf? Will you alwayes hold us in one Lesson? surely you will make Dunces of us; then all the Boyes in other Lands will laugh at us: come, I pray let us take forth, and go forward in our learning.

You blame us who are the Common people as though we would have no government; truly Gentlemen, We desire a righteous government with all our hearts, but the government we have gives freedom and livelihood to the Gentrie, to have abundance, and to lock up Treasures of the Earth from the poor, so that rich men may have chests full of Gold and Silver, and houses full of Corn and Goods to look upon; and the poor that works to get it, can hardly live, and if they cannot work like Slaves, then they must starve. And thus the Law gives all the Land to some part of mankind whose Predecessors got it by conquest, and denies it to others, who by the righteous Law of Creation may claim an equall portion; and yet you say this is a righteous government, but surely it is no other but self-ishness, which is the great Red Dragon the Murtherer.

England is a Prison; the variety of subtilties in the Laws preserved by the Sword, are bolts, bars, and doors of the prison; the Lawyers are the Jaylors, and poor men are the prisoners; for let a man fall into the hands of any from the Bailiffe to the Judge, and he is either undone, or wearie of his life.

Surely this power the Laws, which is the great Idoll that people dote upon, is the burden of the Creation, a Nurserie of Idleness, luxurie, and cheating, the only enemie of Christ the King of righteousness; for though it pretend justice, yet the Judges and Law-Officers, buy and sell Justice for money, and wipes their mouths like *Solomons* whore, and says it is my calling, and never are troubled at it.

Two things must cast out this Idoll: First, Let not people send their children to those Nurseries of Covetousness, *The Innes of Court*. Secondly, let not people live in contention, but fulfill Christs last commandment, *Love;* and endeavour to practice that full point of the Law and the Prophets, *Doe as you would be done by*, and so cast out envie and discontent. Woe to you Lawyers, for your trade is the bane and miserie of the world; your power is the only power that hinders Christ from rising; the destruction of your power will be the life of the World; it is full of confusion, it is Babylon, and surely its fall is neer, in regard the light of truth is rising, who will continue your power, but save your persons by the words of his mouth, and brightnesse of his coming.

The Lawyers trade is one of the false Prophets, that says, Lo here is Christ, Ile save you in this Court, and lo there is Christ, Ile save you in that Court: but when we have tried all, we are lost, and not saved, for we are either utterly made Beggars by this Saviour, the Law, or else we are nursed up in hardnesse of heart and cruelty against our fellow creature whom we ought to love and preserve, and not destroy: This Saviour jeeres righteousness, and bids every man save himself, and never regard what becomes of another, and so is a plain destroyer of the Creation; Surely that Wo pronounced against Lawyers by the Man Christ must be fulfilled, delay is no payment: Therefore you Parliament and Army that have power in your hands, reform the Law; and suffer none to be called to practice Law but reformed ones; nay suffer every man to plead his own cause, and choose his own Lawyer, where he finds the most ingenuous man: Wel, every mans burthen in this Age fills their mouths with words of Lamentation against Law and Lawyers sufficiently; therefore you that have an opportunitie to ease the cry of the oppressed, shut not your eies and eares, but cast out this covetous corruption whereby corrupt Lawyers doe oppress the People; it is another Branch of the Kingly power.

You Gentlemen of *Surrey,* and Lords of Mannors, and you Mr Parson *Platt* especially, that lay almost a fortnight waiting and tempting the Lord *Fairfax* to send Souldiers to drive off the Diggers, when he granted your Desire, it was but to secure the Shereiff, for he did not give them commission to beat us, which we thank him for; and we thank the Souldiers for their moderation, that they would not strike poor wormes, *Englands* and the creations faithfull friends, though you would have moved them thereunto. My Advice to you Gentlemen is this, Hereafter to lie still and cherish the Diggers, for they love you, and would not have your finger ake if they could help it; and why should you be so bitter against them? Oh let them live by you, some of them have been Souldiers, and some countrie-men that were alwayes friends to the Parliaments cause, by whose hardship and meanes you enjoy the creatures about you in peace; and will you now destroy part of them that have preserved your lives? O do not do so; be not so besotted with the Kinglie power; hereafter let not the Attourneyes or Lawyers neatly councel your Money out of your purses, and stir you up to beat and abuse the Diggers, to make all rational men laugh at your folly, and condemn you for your bitterness: If you have yet so much Money give it not away to destroy men, but give it to some poor or other to be a Stock, and bid them go and Plant the common; this will be your honour, and your comfort; assure your selves you never must have true comfort tell you be friends with the poor; therefore come, come, love the Diggers, and make restitution of their Land you from them; for what would you do if you had not such labouring men to work for you?

And you great Officers of the Army and Parliament, love your common Souldiers, (I plead for Equity and Reason) and do not force them by long delay of Payment to sell you their deer bought Debenters for a thing of naught, and then to go and buy our common Land, and crown Land, and other Land that is the spoil one of another, therewith: Remember you are Servants to the commons of *England*, and you were Volunteers in the Wars, and the common people have paid you for your pains so largely, that some of us have not left our selves hardly bread to eat; and therefore if there be a spoil to be gathered of crown Lands, Deans, Bishops, Forrests Lands and commons, that is to come to the poor commons freely; and you ought to be content with your wages, unless you will denie Christ and the Scriptures; and you ought not to go and buy one of another that which is common to all the Nation; for you ought neither to buy nor sell other mens Proprietie by the Law of creation; for Christ gives you no such Warrant. As soon as you have freed the Earth from one intanglement of Kinglie power, will you intangle it more, and worse by another degree of Kinglie power? I pray consider what you do, and do righteously: We that are the poor commons, that paid our Money, and gave you free Quarter, have as much Right in those crown Lands and Lands of the spoil as you;

therefore we give no consent That you should buy and sell our crown Lands and waste Lands, for it is our purchased inheritance from under Oppression, it is our own, even the poor common peoples of *England:* It was taken from us, and hath been held from us by former conquests, whereof the Norman conquest was the last, which is cast out by yours and our joynt Assistance; therefore you cannot in Equity take it from us, nor we cannot in Equity take it from you, for it is our joynt purchased inheritance; we paid you your wages to help us to recover it, but not to take it to your selves, and turn us out, and buy and sell it among your selves; for this is a cheat of the Kinglie swordlie power which you hold up; and we profess to all the world, in so doing you denie God, Christ, and the Scriptures whom ye professed you own: for God, Christ, and Scriptures owne no such practice: Likewise we profess to all the Creation, That in so doing you rob us of our Rights; & you kill us, by denying to give us our livelihood in our own inheritance freely, which is the crown Land and Comon Land and waste Lands, Bishops & Deans, which some of you begin to say you are not satisfied in your conscience to let us have; I, well spoke tender hearted Covetousness; if you do so you will uphold the Kinglie power, and so disobey both Acts of Parliament, and break your Oath, and you will live in the breach of those Two Commandments, *Thou shalt not kill: Thou shalt not steal;* by denying us the Earth which is our Livelyhood, and thereby killing us by a lingring death.

Well, the end of all my Speech is to point out the Kingly power, where I spie it out, and you see it remains strongly in the hands of Lords of Mannors, who have delt discourteously with some who are sincere in heart, though there have some come among the Diggers that have caused scandall, but we dis-own their wayes.

The Lords of Mannors have sent to beat us, to pull down our houses, spoil our labours; yet we are patient, and never offered any violence to them again, this 40 weeks past, but wait upon God with love till their hearts thereby be softened; and all that we desire is, but to live quietly in the land of our nativity, by our righteous labour, upon the common Land which is our own, but as yet the Lords of the Mannor so formerly called, will not suffer us, but abuse us. Is not that part of the Kingly power? In that which follows I shall cleerly prove it is, for it appears so cleer that the understanding of a child does say, It is Tyranny, it is the Kingly power of darkness, therefore we expect that you will grant us the benefit of your Act of Parliament that we may say, Truly *England* is a Common-wealth, and a free people indeed.

Sire, Though your Tithing Priests and others tell you, That we Diggers do deny God, Christ, and the Scripture, to make us odious, and themselves better thought of; yet you will see in time when the King of Righteousness whom we serve does cleer our innocencie, That our actions and conversation is the very life of the Scripture, and holds forth the true power of God and Christ. For is not the end of all preaching, praying, and profession wrapped up in this action, (namely, *Love your enemies, and doe to all men, as you would they should do to you, (or this is the very Law and the Prophets.* This is the New Commandement that Christ left behind him. Now if any seem to say this, and does not do this, but acts contrary, for my part I owne not their wayes, they are members that uphold the curse.

Bare talking of righteousnesse, and not acting, hath ruled, and yet does rule king of darkness in the creation; and it is the cause of all this immoderate confusion and ignorance that is in men.

But the actings of righteousnesse from the inward power of love, shall rule King of righteousnesse to the creation now in these later dayes, and cast the other Serpent and fiery Scorpion out; for this is Christ the restoring power: and as he rises up, so multitude of words without action (which is hypocrisie) is to die, his judgment hastens apace.

If any sort of people hold the earth to themselves by the dark Kingly power, and shut out others from that freedom, they deny God, Christ, and Scriptures, and they overthrow all their preaching praying, and profession; for the Scriptures declare them to be Hypocrites, Scribes and Pharisees, *that say, and do not;* they have words, and no deeds: Like Parson *Platt* the Preacher at *Horsley* in *Surrey,* a Lord of Mannor (by marriage) of the place where we digg, who caused a poor old mans house that stood upon the Common, to be pulled down in the evening of a cold day, and turned the old man, and his wife, and daughter to lie in the open field, because he was a Digger: and he, and other Lords of Mannors, and Gentlemen sent their servants up and down the Town, to bid their Tenants and neighbours, neither to give the Diggers lodging nor victuals., on pain of their displeasure. Though this Parson *Platt* preach the Scriptures, yet I'll affirm, he denyes God,

Christ, and Scriptures, and knowes nothing of them; for covetousness, pride, and envie hath blinded his eyes. A man knowes no more of righteousness than he hath power to act; and surely, this cruelty of preaching *Platt* is an unrighteous act.

If the Diggers were enemies, (oh you Lords of Mannors) as are not, you ought to love them: I am sure, they love you; a you doubt it, put them to the tryall; you shall find them more faithfull than many of those pick-thank slaves, and belly-god servants to whom your ears are open, when they bring tales full of envie to you against us.

We are told likewise, That to make us who are called Diggers odious, and to incense you against us, there came to the Generall and Councell of State, divers Justices, and others, and told you, that we Diggers were Cavaliers, and that we waited an opportunity, and gathered together to stand up for the Prince.

But all that know us can prove that to be a false report, to the dishonour of those justices; for we have been friends to the Parliaments cause, and so do continue, and will continue; for this work of digging, to make *England* a free Common-wealth, is the life and marrow of the Parliaments cause. And the two Acts of Parliament, the One, to cast out Kingly power, the Other, to make *England* a free Common-wealth, declares it: and we do obey those Acts, and will obey them, for they hold forth righteousnesse.

But for our rising in arms for the Prince, or any other, let any come and see our strength and work, and they will say, It is a meer envious slander cast upon us, to incense you against us.

Besides, You shall see by and by, That our principles are wholly against Kingly power in everyone, as well as in one. Likewise we hear that they told you, that the Diggers do steal and rob from others, This likewise is a slander: we have things stollen from us; but if any can prove that any of us do steal any mans proper goods, as Sheep, Geese, Pigs, as they say, let such be made a spectacle to all the world: For my part, I own no such doing, neither do I know any such thing by any of the Diggers. Likewise they report, that we Diggers hold women to be common, and live in that bestialnesse: For my part, I declare against it; I own this to be a truth, That the earth ought to be a common Treasury to all; but as for women, *Let every man have his own wife, and every woman her own husband;* and I know none of the Diggers that act in such an unrationall excesse of female communitie: If any should, I professe to have nothing to do with such people, but leave them to their own Master, who will pay them with torment of minde, and diseases in their bodies.

These and such-like tales, we hear, are brought to you, to incense you against us: but we desire you to mark them that bring them for we partly know who they be, and we can tell them to their faces, they were Cavaliers, and had hands in the Kentish Rising, and in stirring up that offensive *Surrey* Petition, which was the occasion of bloodshed in *Westminster*-yard, and they would rejoyce to see the Prince come in with an Armie to over-top you: for we know, they love you not but from the teeth outwards, for their own ends: And these are the proud *Hamans,* that would incense you against the *Mordecaies* of the Land, even our true-hearted friends, the Diggers. Well, in the midst of our slanders we rejoyce in the uprightness of our hearts, and we do *commit our cause to him that judgeth righteously.*

Upon these lying reports, and importunitie to the General, it seems the General granted the Lords of Mannor to have some souldiers to go along with the Sheriff, to pull down the Diggers houses; and so the souldiers did come: but they were very moderate and rationall men, and as they were sent to secure the Sheriff, so they did: but there was no cause; for, though the Gentlemen possess'd the General, that they feared opposition from the Diggers, yet the souldiers saw they lifted not up a finger in discontent, but fought against those dragons, the Lords of Manors, with the spirit of love and patience: for when the two Lords of Manor sat among the souldiers on horsback and coach, and commanded their fearfull tenants to pull down one of the Diggers houses before their faces, and rejoyced with shouting at the fall; yet some of the Diggers stood by, and were very chearfull, and preached the Gospel to those Turkish *Bashaws,* which are words of life, and in time will prove words of terrour, to torment their awakened consciences.

And the poor tenants that pulled down the house, durst do no other, becuse their Land-lords and Lords looked on, for fear they should be turned out of service, or their livings; as a poor honest man, because he looked with a cheerfull countenance upon the Diggers (though he was affraid to come neer, or affraid to speak openly, lest his Landlords setting-dogs should smell the sound of his words, and carry a pick-thank tale, which his Lords ears are much open to) a Baily was sent presently to him, to warn him out of his house.

Can the Turkish Bashaws hold their slaves in more bondage than these Gospel-professing Lords of Manors do their poor tenants? and is not this the Kingly power? O you rulers of *England*, I pay see that your acts be obeyed, and let the oppressed go free.

And when the poor enforced slaves had pulled down the house, then their Lords gave them ten shillings to drink, and there they smiled one upon another; being fearfull, like a dog that is kept in awe, when his Master gives him a bone, and stands over him with a whip; he will eat, and look up, and twinch his tail; for they durst not laugh out, lest their Lords should hear they jeer'd them openly; for in their hearts they are Diggers. Therefore, you Lords of Manors, if you have none to stand for you but whom you force by threatning, then leave off striving against the spirit, and say you are fallen, and come in and embrace righteousnesse, that you may finde mercy betimes.

The next day after this, there came two souldiers and three Country-men to another house which the Diggers had set up, (which the Sheriff the day before had let alone, for, as some say, he was grieved to see what was done,) one of these souldiers was very civill, and walked lovingly with the Diggers round their corn which they had planted, and commended the work, and would do no harm (as divers others were of the same minde) and when he went his way, gave the Diggers 12 d. to drink: but the other souldier was so rude, that he forced those three Country-men to help him to pull down the house, and railed bitterly: the men were unwilling to pull it down; but for fear of their Landlords, and the threatning souldier, they did put their hands to pull it down.

And seeing Parson *Platt* (the Lord of that Manor) will not suffer the Diggers to have a house, (wherein he forgets his Master Christ, that is persecuted in naked, hungry, and houselesse members) yet the Diggers were mighty cheerfull, and their spirits resolve to wait upon God, to see what he will do, and they have built them some few little hutches like calf-cribs, and there they lie anights, and follow their work adayes still with wonderfull joy of heart, taking the spoyling of their goods cheerfully, counting it a great happinesse to be persecuted for righteoussnesse sake, by the Priests and Professors, that are the successors of *Judas,* and the bitter- spirited Pharisees that put the man Christ *Jesus* to death. And they have planted divers Acres of Wheat and Rye, which is come up, and promises a very hopefull crop, committing their cause to God, and wait upon him, saying, O thou King of righteousnesse, do thine own work.

O that you would search and try our wayes narrowly, and see whether we deny God, Christ, Scriptures, as the Priests slander us we do; and you shall finde, that the Scriptures warrant our action, and God in Christ is the life of our souls, and the support of our spirits in the midst of this our sharp persecution from the hands of unreasonable men, who have not faith in Christ, but uphold the Kingly power, which you have Voted down.

Likewise, you shall see, that we live in the performance of that work which is the very life and marrow of the Parliaments Cause, whereby we honour the Parliament and their Cause: as you shall see by this following Declaration, unfolding the foundation whereupon *Englands* Laws are, or the Freedom of a Common-wealth ought to be built, which is Equity and Reason.

In the time of the Kings, who came in as Conquerors, and ruled by the power of the Sword, not only the Common land, but the Inclosures also were captivated under the will of those Kings, till now of late that our later Kings granted more freedom to the Gentry than they had presently after the conquest; yet under bondage still: for what are prisons, whips and gallows in the times of peace, but the laws and power of the sword, forcing and compelling obedience, and so enslaving, as if the sword raged in the open field?

England was in such a slavery under the Kingly power, that both Gentry and Commonaltie groaned under bondage; and to ease themselves, they endeavoured to call a Parliament, that by their counsels and decrees they might find some freedom.

But *Charles* the then King perceiving that the Freedom they strove for, would derogate from his Prerogative-tyranny, therupon he goes into the North, to raise a War against the Parliament, and took

WILLIAM *the Conqueror's* Sword into his hand again, thereby to keep under the former conquered English, and to uphold his Kingly power of self-will and Prerogative, which was the power got by former Conquests; that is, to rule over the lives and estates of all men at his will, and so to make us pure slaves and vassals.

Well, This Parliament, that did consist of the chief Lords, Lord of Manors, and Gentry, and they seeing that the King, by raising an Army, did thereby declare his intent to enslave all sorts to him by the sword; and being in distresse, and in a low ebb, they call upon the common people to bring in their Plate, Moneys, Taxes Free-quarter, Excise, and to adventure their lives with them, and they would endeavour to recover *England* from that *Norman* yoak, and make us a free people: and the common people assent hereunto, and call this the Parliaments Cause, and own it, and adventure person and purse to preserve it; and by the joynt assistance of Parliament and People, the King was beaten in the field, his head taken off, and his Kingly power voted down; and we the Commons thereby virtually have recovered our selves from the Norman Conquest, we want nothing but posession of the spoyl, which is a free use of the Land for our livelyhood.

And from hence we the common people, or younger brothers plead our propriety in the Common land, as truly our own by vertue of this victory over the King; as our elder brothers can plead proprietie in their Inclosures; and that for three reasons in *Englands* law.

First, By a lawfull purchase or contract between Parliament and us; for they were our Landlords and Lords of Mannors that held the freedom of the Commons from us, while the King was in his power; for they held title thereunto from him, he being the head, and they branches of the Kingly power, that enslaved the people by that ancient Conquerors Sword, that was the ruling power: For they said, Come and help us against the King that enslaves us, that we may be delivered from his Tyranny, and we will make you a free People.

Now they cannot make us free, unlesse they deliver us from the bondage which they themselves held us under; and that is, they held the freedom of the Earth from us: for we in part with them have delivered ourselves from the King: now we claim freedom from that bondage you have, and yet do hold us under, by the bargain and contract between Parliament and us, who (I say) did consist of Lords of Manors, and Landlords, whereof Mr. *Drake,* who hath arrested me for digging upon the Common, was one at that time: Therefore by the law of Bargain and Sale, we claim of them our freedom, to live comfortably with them in this Land of our Nativity; and this we cannot do, so long as we lie under poverty, and must not be suffered to plant the commons and waste land for our livelihood: for, take away the land from any people, and those people are in a way of continuall death and misery; and better not to have had a body, than not to have food and rayment for it. But (I say) they have sold us our freedom in the common, and have been largely paid for it; for by means of our bloods and money, they sit in peace: for if the King had prevailed, they had lost all, and been in slavery to the meanest Cavalier, if the King would. Therfore we the Commons say, Give us our bargain: if you deny us our bargain, you deny God, Christ, and Scriptures; and all your profession then is and hath been hypocrisie.

Secondly, The Commons and Crown land is our propriety by equall conquest over the Kingly power: for the Parl. did never stir up the people by promises and covenant to assist them to cast out the King, and to establish them in the Kings place and prerogative power; No, but all their Declarations were for the safety and peace of the whole Nation.

Therefore the common-people being part of the Nation, and especially they that bore the greatest heat of the day in casting out the oppressor: and the Nation cannot be in peace, so long as the Poor oppressed are in wants, and the land is intangled and held from them by bondage.

But the Victory being obtained over the King, the spoyl which is properly in the Land, ought in equity to be divided now between the two Parties, that is, Parliament and Common-people. The Parliament, consisting of Lords of Manors, and Gentry, ought to have their inclosure Lands free to them without molestation, as they are freed from the Court of Wards.

And the Common-people, consisting of Souldiers, and such as paid Taxes and Free-quarter, ought to have the freedom of all waste and common land, and Crown-land equally among them; the Souldiery ought not in equity to have all, nor the other people paid them to have all; but the spoyle ought to be divided between them that stay'd at home, and them that went to Warr; for the Victory is for the whole Nation.

And as the Parliament declared, they did all for the Nation, and not for themselves onely; so we plead with the Armie, they did not fight for themselves, but for the freedom of the Nation: and I say, we have bought our Freedom of them likewise by Taxes and Free-quarter: therefore we claim an equall Freedom with them in this Conquest over the King.

Thirdly We claim an equall portion in the Victory over the King, by vertue of the two Acts of Parliament, the One to make *England* a Free-Common-wealth; the Other to take away Kingly power. Now the Kingly power (you have heard) is a power that rules by the Sword in covetousnesse and self, giving the earth to some, and denying it to others: and this Kingly power was not in the hand of the King alone; but Lords, and Lords of Manors, and corrupt Judges, and Lawyers especially, held it up likewise; for he was the head, and they, with the Tything-priests are the branches of that Tyrannical Kingly power; and all the several limbs and members must be cast out; before Kingly power can be pulled up root and branch. Mistake me not, I do not say, Cast out the persons of men: No, I do not desire their fingers to ake: but I say, Cast out their power, whereby they hold the people in bondage, as the King held them in bondage. And I say, it is our own Freedom we claim, both by bargain, and by equality in the Conquest; as well as by the Law of righteous Creation, which gives the Earth to all equally.

And the power of Lords of Mannors lies in this: They deny the Common people the use and free benefit of the Earth, unless they give them leave, and pay them for it, either in Rent, in Fines, in Homages, or Heriots. Surely the Earth was never made by God, that the Younger brother should not live in the Earth, unless he would work for, and pay his Elder brother Rent for the Earth: No; this Slavery came in by Conquest, and it is part of the Kingly power; and *England* cannot be a Free Common-wealth, till this Bondage be taken away. You have taken away the King; you have taken away the House of Lords: Now step two steps further, and take away the power of Lords of Mannors, and of Tything Priests, and the intolerable oppressions of Judges, by whom Laws are corrupted; and your work will be honourable.

Fourthly, if this Freedom be denied the Common people, To enjoy the Common Land; then Parliament, Army and Judges will deny Equity and Reason, whereupon the Laws of a well-governed Common-wealth ought to be built: And if this Equity be denied then there can be no Law, but Club-Law, among the people: and if the Sword must raign, then every Party will be striving to bear the Sword; and then farewel Peace; nay, farewel Religion and Gospel, unless it be made use of to intrap one another, as we plainly see some Priests and others make if a Cloke for their Knavery. If I adventure my life, and fruit of my labour, equal with you, and obtain what we strive for; it is both Equity and Reason, that I should equall divide the Spoil with you, and not you to have all, and I none: And if you deny us this, you take away our Propriety from us, our Moneys and Blood, and give us nothing for it.

Therefore, I say, the Common Land is my own Land, equal with my fellow-Commoners; and our true Propriety, by the Law of Creation: it is everyones, but not one single ones: Yea, the Commons are as truely ours by the last excellent two Acts of Parliament, the Foundation of *Englands* new righteous Government aimed at, as the Elder brothers can say the Inclosures are theirs: for they adventured their Lives, and covenanted with us to help them to preserve their Freedom: And we adventured our lives, and they covenanted with us, to purchase and to give us our Freedom, that hath been hundreds of yeers kept from us.

Daemona non Armis, sed Morte subegit Jesus.

By patient Sufferings, not by Death,
Christ did the Devil kill;
And by the same, still to this day,
his Foes he conquers still.

True Religion, and undefiled, is this, To make restitution of the Earth, which hath been taken and held from the Common people, by the power of Conquests formerly, and so *set the oppressed free*. Do not All strive to enjoy the Land? The Gentry strive for Land. the Clergie strive for Land, the Common people strive for Land; and Buying and Selling is an Art, whereby people endeavour to cheat one another of the Land.

Now if any can prove, from the Law of Righteousness, that the Land was made peculiar to him and his successively, shutting others out, he shall enjoy it freely, for my part: But I affirm, It was made for all; and true- Religion is, To let everyone enjoy it. Therefore, you Rulers of *England,* make restitution of the Lands which the Kingly power holds from us: *Set the oppressed free;* and come in, and honour Christ, who is the Restoring Power, and you shall finde rest.

A LETTER TO THE LORD FAIRFAX

AND HIS COUNCELL OF WAR, WITH *Divers Questions to the Lawyers, and Ministers:* Proving it an undeniable Equity, That the common People ought to dig, plow, plant and dwell upon the Commons, with-out hiring them, or paying Rent to any.

Delivered to the Generall and the chief Officers on Saturday June 9.

To the Lord Fairfax, *Generall of the English Forces, and his Councell of War.*

SIR,

Our digging and ploughing upon George-hill in Surrey is not unknown to you, since you have seen some of our persons, and heard us speak in defence thereof: and we did receive mildnesse and moderation from you and your Councell of Warre, both when some of us were at White-hall before you, and when you came in person to George-hill to view our works; we indeavour to lay open the bottome and intent of our businesse, as much as can be, that none may be troubled with doubtfull imaginations about us, but may be satisfied in the sincerity and universall righteousnesse of the work.

We understand, that our digging upon that Common, is the talk of the whole Land; some approving, some disowning, some are friends, filled with love, and sees the worke intends good to the Nation, the peace whereof is that which we seeke after; others are enemies filled with fury, and falsely report of us, that we have intent to fortifie our selves, and afterwards to fight against others, and take away their goods from them, which is a thing we abhor: and many other slanders we rejoyce over, because we know ourselves cleare, our endeavour being not otherwise, but to improve the Commons, and to cast off that oppression and outward bondage which the Creation groans under, as much as in us lies, and to lift up and preserve the purity thereof.

And the truth is, experience shews us, that in this work of Community in the earth, and in the fruits of the earth, is seen plainly a pitched battaile between the Lamb and the Dragon, between the Spirit of love, humility and righteousnesse, which is the Lamb appearing in flesh; and the power of envy, pride, and unrighteousnesse, which is the Dragon appearing in flesh, the latter power striving to hold the Creation under slavery, and to lock and hide the glory thereof from man: the former power labouring to deliver the Creation from slavery, to unfold the secrets of it to the Sons of Men, and so to manifest himselfe to be the great restorer of all things.

And these two powers strive in the heart of every single man, & make single men to strive in opposition one against the other, and these strivings will be till the Dragon be cast out, and his judgement and downfall hastens apace, therefore let the righteous hearts wait with patience upon the Lord, to see what end he makes of all the confused hurley burleys of the world.

When you were at our Works upon the Hill, we told you, many of the Countrey-people that were offended at first, begin now to be moderate, and to see righteousnesse in our work, and to own it, excepting one or two covetous Free-holders, that would have all the Commons to themselves, and that would uphold the Norman Tyranny over us, which by the victorie that you have got over the Norman Successor, is plucked up by the roots, therefore ought to be cast away. And we expect, that these our angry neighbours, whom we never wronged, nor will not wrong, will in time see their furious rashnesse to be their folly, and become moderate, to speak and carry themselves like men rationafiy, and leave off pushing with their hornes like beasts: they shall have no cause to say wee wrong them, unlesse they count us wrongers of them for seeking a livelihood out of the common Land of England by our righteous labour, which is our freedome, as we are Englishmen equall with them, and rather our freedome then theirs, because they are elder brothers and Free-holders, and call the Inclosures their own land, and we are younger brothers, and the poore oppressed, and the Common Lands are called ours, by their owne confession.

We told you (upon a question you put to us) that we were not against any that would have Magistrates and Laws to govern, as the Nations of the world are governed, but as for our parts we shall need neither the one nor the other in that nature of Government; for as our Land is common, so our Cattell is to be common, and our corn and fruits of the earth common, and are not to be bought and sold among us, but to remaine a standing portion of livelihood to us and our children, without that cheating intanglement of buying and selhng, and we shall not arrest one another.

And then, what need have we of imprisoning, whipping, or hanging Laws, to bring one another into bondage? and we know that none of those that are subject to this righteous law dares arrest or inslave his brother for, or about the objects of the earth, because the earth is made by our Creator to be a common Treasury of livelihood to one equall with another, without resect of persons.

But now if you that are elder brothers, and that call the Inclosures your own land, hedging out others, if you will have Magistrates and Laws in this outward manner of the Nations, we are not against it, but freely without disturbance shall let you alone; and if any of we Commoners, or younger Brothers, shall steal your corne, or cattell, or pull down your hedges, let your laws take hold upon any of us that so offends.

But while we keep within the bounds of our Commons, and none of us shall be found guilty of medling with your goods, or inclosed proprieties, unlesse the Spirit in you freely give it up, your laws then shall not reach to us, unlesse you will oppresse or shed the blood of the innocent: and yet our corn and cattell shall not be locked up, as though we would be proprietors in the middle of the Nation: no, no, we freely declare, that our corn and cattell, or what we have, shall be freely laid open, for the safety and preservation of the Nation, and we as younger brothers, living in love with you our elder brothers, for we shall endeavour to do, as we would be done unto; that is, to let everyone injoy the benefit of his Creation, to have food and rayment free by the labour of his hands from the earth.

And as for spirituall teachings, we leave every man to stand and fall to his own Master: if the power of covetousnesse be his Master or King that rules in his heart, let him stand and fall to him; if the power of love and righteousnesse be his Master or King that rules in his heart, let him stand and fall to him; let the bodies of men act love, humility, and righteousnesse one towards another, and let the Spirit of righteousnesse be the Teacher, Ruler and Judge both in us and over us; and by thus doing, we shall honor our Father, the Spirit that gave us our being. And we shall honor our Mother the earth, by labouring her in righteousnesse, and leaving her free from oppression and bondage.

We shall then honour the higher powers of the left hand man, which is our hearing, seeing, tasting, smelling, feeling, and walk in the light of reason and righteousnesse, that is, the King and Judge that sits upon this five cornered Throne, and we shall be strengthened by those five well springs of life, of the right hand man, which is, understanding, will, affections, joy and peace, and so live like men, in the light and power of the Son of righteousnesse within our selves feelingly. What need then have we of any outward, selfish, confused Laws made, to uphold the power of covetousnesse, when as we have the righteous Law written in our hearts, teaching us to walk purely in the Creation.

Sir, The intent of our writing to you, is not to request your protection, though we have received an unchristian-like abuse from some of your souldiers; for truly we dare not cast off the Lord, and make choice of a man or men to rule us. For the Creation hath smarted deeply for such a thing, since Israel chose Saul to be their King; therefore we acknowledge before you in plain English, That we have chosen the Lord God Almighty to be our King and Protector.

Yet in regard you are our brethren (as an English Tribe) and for the present are owned to be the outward Governors, Protectors and Saviours of this Land, and whose hearts we question not, but that you endeavour to advance the same King of righteousnesse with us, therefore we are free to write to you, and to open the sincerity of our hearts freely to you, and to all the world.

And if after this report of ours, either you, or your Forces called souldiers, or any that owns your Laws of propriety, called freeholders, do abuse or kill our persons, we declare to you that we die, doing our duty to our Creator, by endeavouring from that power he hath put into our hearts to lift up his Creation out of bondage, and you and they shall be left without excuse in the day of Judgement, because you have been spoken to sufficiently.

And therefore our reason of writing to you is this, in regard some of your foot souldiers of the Ceneralls Regiment, under Captain Stravie that were quartered in our Town, we bearing part therein as well as our neighbours, giving them sufficient quarter, so that there was no complaining, did notwithstanding, go up to George-hill, where was onely one man and one boy of our company of the diggers. And at their first coming, divers of your souldiers, before any word of provocation was spoken to them, fell upon those two, beating the boy, and took away his coat off his back, and some linnen and victualls that they had, beating and wounding the man very dangerously, and fired our house.

Which we count a strange and Heathenish practise, that the souldierie should meddle with naked men, peaceable men, Countrymen, that meddled not with the souldiers businesse, nor offered any wrong to them in word or deed, uniesse, because we improve that victory which you have gotten in the name of the Commons over King Charles, do offend the souldierie. In doing whereof, we rather expect protection from you then destruction. But for your own particular, we are assured of your moderation and friendship to us, who have ever been your friends in times of straits; and that you would not give Commission to strike us, or fire and pull down our houses, but you would prove us an enemy first.

Yet we do not write this, that you should lay any punishment upon them, for that we leave to your discretion, only we desire (in the request of brethren) that you would send forth admonition to your souldiers, not to abuse us hereafter; unlesse they have a Commission from you; and truly if our offences should prove so great, you shall not need to send souldiers for us, or to beat us, for we shall freely come to you upon a bare letter.

Therefore that the ignorant, covetous, free-holders, and such of your ignorant souldiers, that know not what freedom is, may not abuse those that are true friends to Englands freedom, and faithfull servants to the Creation, we desire, that our businesse may be taken notice of by you, and the highest Councell the Parliament, and if our work appear righteous to you, as it does to us, and wherein our souls have sweet peace, in the midst of scandalls and abuses;

Then in the request of brethren, we desire we may injoy our freedom, according to the Law of contract between you and us, That we that are younger brothers, may live comfortably in the Land of our Nativity, with you the elder brothers, enjoying the benefit of our Creation, which is food and rayment freely by our labours; and that we may receive love, and the protection of brethren from you, seeing we have adventured estate and persons with you, to settle the Land in peace, and that we may not be abused by your Laws, nor by your souldiers, unlesse we break over into your inclosures as aforesaid, and take away your proprieties, before you are willing to deliver it up. And if this you do, we shall live in quietnesse, and the Nation will be brought into peace, while you that are the souldierie, are a wall of fire round about the Nation to keep a forraign enemy, and are succourers of your brethren that live within the Land, who indeavour to hold forth the Sun of righteousnesse in their actions, to the glory of our Creator.

And you and the Parliament hereby, will be faithfull in your Covenants, Oaths and promises to us, as we have been faithfull to you and them, in paying taxes, giving free-quarter, and affording other assistance in the publike work, whereby we that are the Common People, are brought almost to a morsell of bread, therefore we demand our bargain, which is freedome, with you in this Land of our Nativity.

But if you do sleight us and our cause, then know we shall not strive with sword and speare, but with spade and plow and such like instruments to make the barren and common Lands fruitful, and we have, and still shall, commit our selves and our cause unto our righteous King, whom we obey, even the Prince of peace to be our Protector; and unto whom you likewise professe much love, by your preaching, praying, fastings, and in whose name you have made all your Covenants, Oaths, and promises to us: I say unto him we appeal, who is and will be our righteous Judge, who never yet failed those that waited upon him, but ever did judge the cause of the oppressed righteously.

We desire that your Lawyers may consider these questions (which we affirm to be truths) and which gives good assurance by the Law of the

Land, that we that are the younger brothers or common people, have a true right to dig, plow up and dwell upon the Commons, as we have declared.

1. Whether William the Conqueror became not to be King of England by conquest, turned the English out of their birth-rights, burned divers townes, whereof thirty towns were burned by him in Windsore Forrest; by reason whereof all sorts of people suffered, and compelled the conquered English for necessity of livelihood to be servants to him and his Norman souldiers?

2. Whether King Charles was not successor to the Crown of England from William the Conqueror, and whether all Laws that have been made in every Kings Reign, did not confirm and strengthen the power of the Norman Conquest, and so did, and does still hold the Commons of England under slavery to the Kingly power, his Gentry and Clergie?

3. Whether Lords of Mannours were not the successors of the Colonells and chief Officers of William the Conqueror, and held their Royalty to the Commons by Lease, Grant and Patentee from the King, and the power of the sword was and is the seale to their Title?

4. Whether Lords of Mannours have not lost their Royalty to the common land, since the common People of England, as well as some of the Gentry, have conquered King Charles, and recovered themselves from under the Norman Conquest?

5. Whether the Norman Conqueror took the land of England to himself, out of the hands of a few men, called a Parliament, or from the whole body of the English People? Surely he took freedom from everyone, and became the disposer both of inclosures and commons; therefore everyone, upon the recovery of the conquest, ought to return into freedom again without respecting persons, or els what benefit shall the common people have (that have suffered most in these wars) by the victory that is got over the King? It had been better for the common people there had been no such conquest; for they are impoverished in their estates by Free-quarter and Taxes, and made worse to live then they were before. But seeing they have paid Taxes, and given Free-quarter according to their estates, as much as the Gentry to theirs, it is both reason and equity that they should have the

freedom of the land for their livelihood, which is the benefit of the commons, as the Gentry hath the benefit of their inclosures.

6. Whether the freedom which the common people have got, by casting out the Kingly power, lie not herein principally, to have the land of their nativity for their livelihood, freed from intanglement of Lords, Lords of Mannours, and Landlords, which are our task-masters. As when the enemy conquered England, he took the land for his own, and called that his freedom; even so, seeing all sorts of people have given assistance to recover England from under the Norman yoke, surely all sorts, both Gentry in their inclosures, Commonalty in their Commons, ought to have their freedom, not compelling one to work for wages for another.

7. Whether any Lawes since the coming in of Kings, have been made in the light of the righteous law of our creation, respecting all alike, or have not been grounded upon selfish principles, in feare or flattery of their King, to uphold freedom in the Gentry and Clergie, and to hold the common people under bondage still, and so respecting persons?

8. Whether all Lawes that are not grounded upon equity and reason, not giving a universal freedom to all, but respecting persons, ought not to be cut off with the Kings head? we affirm they ought. If all lawes be grounded upon equity and reason, then the whole land of England is to be a common treasury to everyone that is born in the land: But if they be grounded upon selfish principles, giving freedom to some, laying burdens upon others, such lawes are to be cut off with the Kings head; or els the negiecters are Covenant, Oaths and Promise- breakers, and open hypocrites to the whole world.

9. Whether everyone without exception, by the law of contract, ought not to have liberty to enjoy the earth for his livelihood, and to settle his dwelling in any part of the Commons of England, without buying or renting Land of any; seeing everyone by Agreement and Covenant among themselves, have paid taxes, given free-quarter, and adventured their lives to recover England out of bondage? we affirm, they ought.

10. Whether the Laws that were made in the daies of the Kings, does give freedom to any other people, but to the gentry and Clergy, all the rest are left servants and bondmen to those task~masters; none have

freedom by the Laws, but those two sorts of people, all the common people have been, and still are burdened under them.

And surely if the common people have no more freedom in England, but only to live among their elder brothers, and work for them for hire; what freedom then have they in England, more then we can have in Turkie of France? For there, if any man will work for wages, he may live among them, otherwise no: therefore consider, whether this be righteous, and for the peace of the Nation, that Laws shall be made to give freedom to impropriators and Free-holders, when as the poor that have no land, are left still in the straights of beggery, and are shut out of all livelihood, but what they shall pick out of sore bondage, by working for others, as Masters over them, and if this be not the burthen of the Norman yoke, let rationall men judge: therefore take not away men, but take away the power of tyranny and bad government, the price is in your hand, and let no part of the Nation be wronged for want of a Representative.

And here now we desire your publike Preachers, that say they preach the righteous law, to consider these questions, which confirms us in the peace of our hearts, that we that are the common people born in England, ought to improve the Commons, as we have declared, for a publike Treasury and livelihood, and that those that hinder us are rebelis to their Maker, and enemies to the Creation.

First, we demand I or No, whether the earth with her fruits, was made to be bought and sold from one to another? and whether one part of mankind was made a Lord of the land, and another part a servant, by the law of Creation before the fall?

I affirme, (and I challenge you to disprove) that the earth was made to be a common Treasury of livelihood for all, without respect of persons, and was not made to be bought and sold: And that mankind in all his branches, is the lord over the Beasts, Birds, Fishes, and the Earth, and was not made to acknowledge any of his owne kind to be his teacher and ruler, but the spirit of righteousnesse only his Maker, and to walk in his light, and so to live in peace, and this being a truth, as it is, then none ought to be Lords or Landlords over another, but the earth is free for every son and daughter of mankind, to live free upon.

This question is not to be answered by any text of Scripture, or example since the fall, but the answer is to be given in the light of it self, which is the law of righteousnesse, or that Word of God that was in the beginning, which dwells in mans heart, and by which he was made, even the pure law of creation, unto which the creation is to be restored.

Before the fall, Adam, or the Man did dresse the garden, or the earth, in love, freedom, and righteousnesse, which was his rest and peace: But when covetousnesse began to rise up in him, to kill the power of love and freedom in him, and so made him (mankind) to set himself one man above another, as Cain lifted up himself above Abel, which was but the outward declaration of the two powers that strive in the man Adattis heart; and when he consented to that serpent covetousnesse, then he fell from righteousnesse, was cursed, and was sent into the earth to eat his bread in sorrow: And from that time began particular propriety to grow in one man over another; and the sword brought in propriety, and holds it up, which is no other but the power of angry covetousnesse: For, Cain killed Abel, because Abels principles, or religion, was contrary to his. And the power of the sword is still Cain killing Abel, lifting up one man still above another. But Abel shall not alwaies be slain, nor alwaies lie under the bondage of Cains cursed propriety, for he must rise: And that Abel of old was but a type of Christ, that is now rising up to restore all things from bondage.

2. I demand, whether all wars, blood-shed, and misery came not upon the Creation, when one man indeavoured to be a lord over another, and to claime propriety in the earth one above another? your Scripture will prove this sufficiently to be true. And whether this misery shall not remove (and not till then) when all the branches of mankind shall look upon themselves as one man, and upon the earth as a common Treasury to all, without respecting persons, everyone acknowledging the law of righteousnesse in them and over them, and walking in his light purely? then cast away your buying and selling the earth, with her fruits, it is unrighteous, it lifts up one above another, it makes one man oppresse another, and is the burthen of the Creation.

3. Whether the work of restoration lies not in removing covetousnesse, casting that Serpent out of heaven, (mankind) and making man to live

in the fight of righteousnesse, not in words only, as Preachers do, but in action, whereby the Creation shines in glory? I affirm it.

4. Whether is the King of righteousnesse a respecter of persons yea, or no? If you say no, then who makes this difference, that the elder brother shall be lord of the land, and the younger brother a slave and beggar? I affirm, it was and is covetousnesse, since the fall, not the King of righteousnesse before the fall, that made that difference; therefore if you will be Preachers, hold forth the law of righteousnesse purely, and not the confused law of covetousnesse, which is the murtherer: the law of righteousnesse would have everyone to injoy the benefit of his creation, that is, to have food and rayment by his labour freely in the land of his nativity, but covetousnesse will have none to live free, but he that hath the strongest arme of flesh; all others must be servants.

5. Whether a man can have true peace by walking in the Law of covetousnesse and self, as generally all do, or by walking in the Law of universall righteousnesse; doing as he would be done by? I affirm there is no true peace, till men talk lesse, and live more actually in the power of universall righteousnesse. Then you Preachers, lay aside your multitude of words, and your selfish doctrines, for you confound and delude the people.

6. Whether does the King of righteousnesse bid you love or hate your enemies, if you say love them, then I demand of you, why do some of you in your Pulpits, and elsewhere, stir up the people to beat, to imprison, put to death or banish, or not to buy and sell with those that endeavour to restore the earth to a common treasury again? surely at the worst, you can make them but your enemies; therefore love them, win them by love, do not hate them, they do not hate you.

7. Whether it be not a great breach of the Nationall Covenant, to give two sorts of people their freedom, that is, Gentry and Clergy, and deny it to the rest? I affirm it is a high breach, for mans Laws makes these two sorts of people, the Antichristian task-masters over the common people. The one forcing the people to give them rent for the earth, and to work for hire for them. The other which is the Clergy, that force a maintenance of tithes from the people; a practise which Christ, the

Apostles and Prophets never walked in; therefore surely you are the false Christs, and false Prophets, that are risen up in these latter daies.

Thus I have declared to you, and to all in the whole world, what that power of life is, that is in me. And knowing that the Spirit of righteousnesse does appear in many in this Land, I desire all of you seriously in love and humility, to consider of this businesse of publike community, which I am carried forth in the power of love, and clear light of universall righteousnesse, to advance as much as I can; and I can do no other, the Law of love in my heart does so constrain me, by reason whereof I am called fool, mad man, and have many slanderous reports cast upon me, and meet with much fury from some covetous people, under all which my spirit is made patient, & is guarded with joy and peace: I hate none, I love all, I delight to see everyone live comfortably. I would have none live in poverty, straits or sorrows; therefore if you find any selfishnesse in this work, or discover any thing that is destructive to the whole Creation, that you would open your hearts as freely to me in declaring my weaknesse to me, as I have been open-hearted in declaring that which I find and feel much life and strength in. But if you see righteousnesse in it, and that it holds forth the strength of universall love to all without respect to persons, so that our Creator is honored in the work of his hand, then own it, and justifie it, and let the power of love have his freedom and glory.

Gerrard Winstanly.

The Reformation that England now is to endeavour, is not to remove the Norman Yoke only, and to bring us back to be governed by those Laws that were before William the Conqueror came in, as if that were the rule or mark we aime at: No, that is not it; but the Reformation is according to the Word of God, and that is the pure Law of righteousnesse before the fall, which made all things, unto which all things are to be restored: and he that endeavours not that, is a Covenant-breaker.

This Letter with the Questions were delivered by the Authors own hand to the Generall, and the chief Officers, and they very mildly promised they would read it, and consider of it.

The Law of Freedom in a Nutshell or True Majesty Revealed

To His Excellency Oliver Cromwell

Sir,

God hath honoured you with the highest honour of any man since Moses's time, to be the head of a people who have cast out an oppressing Pharaoh. For when the Norman power had conquered our forefathers, he took the free use of our English ground from them, and made them his servants. And God hath made you a successful instrument to cast out that conqueror, and to recover our land and liberties again, by your victories, out of that Norman hand.

That which is yet wanting on your part to be done is this, to see the oppressor's power to be cast out with his person; and to see that the free possession of the land and liberties be put into the hands of the oppressed commoners of England.

For the crown of honour cannot be yours, neither can those victories be called victories on your part, till the land and freedoms won be possessed by them who adventured person and purse for them.

Now you know, Sir, that the kingly conqueror was not beaten by you only as you are a single man, nor by the officers of the Army joined to you, but by the hand and assistance of the commoners, whereof some came in person and adventured their lives with you; others stayed at home and planted the earth and paid taxes and free-quarter to maintain you that went to war.

So that whatsoever is recovered from the conqueror is recovered by a joint consent of the commoners: therefore it is all equity, that all the commoners who assisted you should be set free from the conqueror's power with you: as David's law was, The spoil shall be divided between them who went to war, and them who stayed at home.

And now you have the power of the land in your hand, you must do one of these two things: first, either set the land free to the oppressed commoners who assisted you and paid the Army their wages; and then you will fulfil the Scriptures and your own engagements, and so take possession of r your deserved honour:

Or secondly, you must only remove the conqueror's power out of the King's hand into other men's, maintaining the old laws still; and then your wisdom and honour is blasted for ever, and you will either lose yourself, or lay the foundation of greater slavery to posterity than you ever knew.

You know that while the King was in the height of his oppressing power, the people only whispered in private chambers against him: but afterwards it was preached upon the house-tops that he was a tyrant and a traitor to England's peace; and he had his overturn.

The righteous power in the creation is the same still. If you and those in power with you should be found walking in the King's steps, can you secure yourselves or posterities from an overturn? Surely no.

The spirit of the whole creation (who is God) is about the reformation of the world, and he will go forward in his work. For if he would not spare kings who have sat so long at his right hand governing the world, neither will he regard you, unless your ways be found more righteous than the King's.

You have the eyes of the people all the land over, nay I think I may say all neighbouring nations over, waiting to see what you will do. And the eyes of your oppressed friends who lie yet under kingly power are waiting to have the possession given them of that freedom in the land which was promised by you, if in case you prevailed. Lose not your crown; take it up and wear it. But know that it is no crown of honour, till promises and engagements made by you be performed to your friends. He that continues to the end shall receive the crown. Now you do not see the end of your work unless the kingly law and power be removed as well as his person.

Jonah's gourd is a remembrancer to men in high places.

The worm in the earth gnawed the root and the gourd died, and Jonah was offended.

Sir, I pray bear with me; my spirit is upon such a lock that I must speak plain to you, lest it tell me another day, 'If thou hadst spoke plain, things might have been amended'.

The earth wherein your gourd grows is the commoners of England.

The gourd is that power which covers you, which will be established to you by giving the people their true freedoms, and not otherwise.

The root of your gourd is the heart of the people, groaning under kingly bondage and desiring a commonwealth's freedom in their English earth.

The worm in the earth, now gnawing at the root of your gourd, is discontents, because engagements and promises made to them by such as have power are not kept.

And this worm hath three heads. The first is a spirit waiting opportunities till a blasting wind arise to cause your gourd to wither; and yet pretends fair to you, etc.

Another spirit shelters under your gourd for a livelihood, and will say as you say in all things; and these are called honest, yet no good friends to you nor the commonwealth, but to their own bellies.

There is a third spirit, which is faithful indeed and plain-dealing, and many times for speaking truth plainly he is cashiered, imprisoned and crushed: and the oppressions laid upon this spirit kindles the fire which the two former waits to warm themselves at.

Would you have your gourd stand for ever? Then cherish the root in the earth, that is the heart of your friends, the oppressed commoners of England, by killing the worm. And nothing will kill this worm but performance of professions, words and promises, that they may be made free men from tyranny.

It may be you will say to me, 'What shall I do?' I answer, 'You are in place and power to see all burdens taken off from your friends, the commoners of England.' You will say, 'What are those burdens?'

I will instance in some, both which I know in my own experience and which I hear the people daily complaining of and groaning under, looking upon you and waiting for deliverance.

Most people cry, 'We have paid taxes, given free-quarter, wasted our estates and lost our friends in the wars, and the task-masters multiply over us more than formerly.' I have asked divers this question, 'Why do you say so?'

Some have answered me that promises, oaths and engagements have been made as a motive to draw us to assist in the wars; that privileges of Parliament and liberties of subjects should be preserved, and that all popery and episcopacy and tyranny should be rooted out; and these promises are not performed. Now there is an opportunity to perform them.

For first, say they, 'The current of succeeding Parliaments is stopped, which is one of the great privileges (and people's liberties) for safety and peace; and if that continue stopped, we shall be more offended by an hereditary Parliament than we were oppressed by an hereditary king'.

And for the commoners, who were called subjects while the kingly conqueror was in power, have not as yet their liberties granted them: I will instance them in order, according as the common whisperings are among the people.

For, they say, the burdens of the clergy remains still upon us, in a threefold nature.

First, if any man declare his judgment in the things of God contrary to the clergy's report or the mind of some high officers, they are cashiered, imprisoned, crushed and undone, and made sinners for a word, as they were in the pope's and bishops' days; so that though their names be cast out, yet their High Commission Court's power remains still, persecuting men for conscience' sake when their actions are unblameable.

Secondly, in many parishes there are old formal ignorant episcopal priests established; and some ministers who are bitter enemies to commonwealth's freedom and friends to monarchy are established preachers, and are continually buzzing their subtle principles into the minds of the people, to undermine the peace of our declared commonwealth, causing a disaffection of spirit among neighbours, who otherwise would live in peace.

Thirdly, the burden of tithes remains still upon our estates, which was taken from us by the kings and given to the clergy to maintain them by our labours; so that though their preaching fill the minds of many with madness, contention and unsatisfied doubting, because their imaginary and ungrounded doctrines cannot be understood by them, yet we must pay them large tithes for so doing. This is oppression.

Fourthly, if we go to the lawyer, we find him to sit in the conqueror's chair though the kings be removed, maintaining the kings' power to the height; for in many courts and cases of law the will of a judge and lawyer rules above the letter of the law, and many cases and suits are lengthened to the great vexation of the clients and to the lodging of their estates in the purse of the unbounded lawyer. So that we see, though other men be under a sharp law, yet many of the great lawyers are not, but still do act their will as the conqueror did; as I have heard some belonging to the law say, 'What cannot we do?'

Fifthly, say they, if we look upon the customs of the law itself, it is the same it was in the kings' days, only the name is altered; as if the commoners of England had paid their taxes, free-quarter and shed their blood not to reform but to baptize the law into a new name, from kingly law to state law; by reason whereof the spirit of discontent is strengthened, to increase more suits of law than formerly was known to be. And so, as the sword pulls down kingly power with one hand, the kings' old law builds up monarchy again with the other.

And indeed the main work of reformation lies in this, to reform the clergy, lawyers and law; for all the complaints of the land are wrapped up within them three, not in the person of a king.

Shall men of other nations say that notwithstanding all those rare wits in the Parliament and Army of England, yet they could not reform the clergy, lawyer and law, but must needs establish all as the kings left them?

Will not this blast all our honour, and make all monarchical members laugh in their sleeves, to see the government of our commonwealth to be built upon the kingly laws and principles?

I have asked divers soldiers what they fought for; they answered, they could not tell; and it is very true, they cannot tell indeed, if the monarchical law be established without reformation. But I wait to see what will be done; and I doubt not but to see our commonwealth's government to be built upon his own foundation.

Sixthly, if we look into Parishes, the burdens there are many.

First, for the power of lords of manors remains still over their brethren, requiring fines and heriots; beating them off the free use of the common land, unless their brethren will pay them rent; exacting obedience as much as they did, and more, when the King was in power.

Now saith the people, 'By what power do these maintain their title over us! 'Formerly they held title from the King, as he was the conqueror's successor. But have not the commoners cast out the King, and broke the bond of that conquest? Therefore in equity they are free from the slavery of that lordly power.

Secondly, in parishes where commons lie, the rich Norman freeholders, or the new (more covetous) gentry, over-stock the commons with sheep and cattle; so that inferior tenants and poor labourers can hardly keep a cow, but half starve her. So that the poor are kept poor still, and the common freedom of the earth is kept from them, and the poor have no more relief than they had when the king (or conqueror) was in power.

Thirdly, in many parishes two or three of the great ones bears all the sway in making assessments, over-awing constables and other officers; and when time was to quarter soldiers, they would have a hand in that, to ease themselves and over-burden the weaker sort; and many times make large sums of money over and above the justice's warrant in assessments, and would give no account why, neither durst the inferior people demand an account, for he that spake should be sure to be crushed the next opportunity; and if any have complained to committees or justices, they have been either wearied out by delays and waiting, or else the offence hath been by them smothered up; so that we see one great man favoured another, and the poor oppressed have no relief.

Fourthly, there is another grievance which the people are much troubled at, and that is this: country people cannot sell any corn or other fruits of the earth in a market town but they must either pay toll or be turned out of town. Now say they, 'This is a most shameful thing, that we must part with our estates in taxes and free-quarter to purchase the freedom of the land and the freedom of the towns, and yet this freedom must be still given from us into the hands of a covetous Norman toll-taker, according to the kings' old burdensome laws, and contrary to the liberty of a free commonwealth.'

'Now,' saith the whisperings of the people, 'the inferior tenants and labourers bears all the burdens, in labouring the earth, in paying taxes and free-quarter beyond their strength, and in furnishing the armies with soldiers, who bear the greatest burden of the war; and yet the gentry, who oppress them and that live idle upon their labours, carry away all the comfortable livelihood of the earth.'

For is not this a common speech among the people? 'We have parted with our estates, we have lost our friends in the wars, which we willingly gave up, because freedom was promised us; and now in the end we have new task-masters, and our old burdens increased: and though all sorts- of people have taken an Engagement to cast out kingly power, yet kingly power remains in power still in the hands of those who have no more right to the earth than ourselves.

'For,' say the people, 'if the lords of manors and our taskmasters hold title to the earth over us from the old kingly power, behold that power is beaten and cast out.

'And two acts of Parliament are made: the one to cast out kingly power, backed by the Engagement against King and House of Lords, the other to make England a free commonwealth.

'And if lords of manors lay claim to the earth over us from the Army's victories over the King, then we have as much right to the land as they, because our labours and blood and death of friends were the purchasers of the earth's freedom as well as theirs.

'And is not this a slavery,' say the people, 'that though there be land enough in England to maintain ten times as many people as are in it, yet some must beg of their brethren, or work in hard drudgery for day wages for them, or starve or steal and so be hanged out of the way, as men not fit to live in the earth, before they must be suffered to plant the waste land for their livelihood, unless they will pay rent to their brethren for it?' Well, this is a burden the creation groans under; and the subjects (so called) have not their birthright freedoms granted them from their brethren, who hold it from them by dub law, but not by righteousness.

'And who now must we be subject to, seeing the conqueror is gone?'

I answer, we must either be subject to a law, or to men's wills. If to a law, then all men in England are subjects, or ought to be, thereunto: but what law that is to which everyone ought to be subject is not yet established in execution. If any say the old kings' laws are the rule, then it may be answered that those laws are so full of confusion that few knows when they obey and when not, because they were the laws of a conqueror to hold the people in subjection to the will of the conqueror; therefore that cannot be the rule for everyone. Besides, we daily see many actions done by state officers, which they have no law to justify them in but their prerogative will.

And again if we must be subject to men, then what men must we be subject to, seeing one man hath as much right to the earth as another, for no man now stands as a conqueror over his brethren by the law of righteousness?

You will say, 'We must be subject to the ruler'. It is true, but not to suffer the rulers to call the earth theirs and not ours, for by so doing they betray their trust and run into the line of tyranny; and we lose our freedom and from thence enmity and wars arise.

A ruler is worthy double honour when he rules well, that tis, when he himself is subject to the law, and requires all others to be subject thereunto, and makes it his work to see the laws obeyed and not his own will; and such rulers are faithful, and they are to be subjected unto us therein, for all commonwealth's rulers are servants to, not lords and kings over, the people. But you will say, 'Is not the land your brother's?

And you cannot take away another man's right by claiming a share therein with him.'

I answer, it is his either by creation right, or by right of conquest. If by creation right he call the earth his and not mine, then it is mine as well as his; for the spirit of the whole creation, who made us both, is no respecter of persons.

And if by conquest he call the earth his and not mine, it must be either by the conquest of the kings over the commoners, or by the conquest of the commoners over the kings.

If he claim the earth to be his from the kings' conquest, the kings are beaten and cast out, and that title is undone.

If he claim title to the earth to be his from the conquest of the commoners over the kings, then I have right to the land as well as my brother, for my brother without me, nor I without my brother, did not cast out the kings; but both together assisting with person and purse we prevailed, so that I have by this victory as equal a share in the earth which is now redeemed as my brother by the law of righteousness.

If my brother still say he will be landlord (through his covetous ambition) and I must pay him rent, or else I shall not live in the land, then does he take my right from me, which I have purchased by my money in taxes, free-quarter and blood. And O thou spirit of the whole creation, who hath this title to be called King of righteousness and Prince of Peace: judge thou between my brother and me, whether this be righteous, etc.

'And now', say the people, 'is not this a grievous thing that our brethren that will be landlords, right or wrong, will make laws and call for a law to be made to imprison, crush, nay put to death, any that denies God, Christ and Scripture; and yet they will not practise that golden rule, Do to another as thou wouldst have another do to thee, which God, Christ and Scriptures hath enacted for a law? Are not these men guilty of death by their own law, which is the words of their own mouth? Is it not a flat denial of God and Scripture?'

O the confusion and thick darkness that hath over-spread our brethren is very great. I have no power to remove it, but lament it in the secrets of my heart. When I see prayers, sermons, fasts, thanksgiving, directed to this God in words and shows, and when I come to look for actions of obedience to the righteous law, suitable to such a profession, I find them men of another nation, saying and not doing; like an old courtier saying 'Your servant', when he was an enemy. I will say no more, but groan and wait for a restoration.

Thus, Sir, I have reckoned up some of those burdens which the people groan under.

And I being sensible hereof was moved in myself to present this platform of commonwealth's government unto you, wherein I have declared a full commonwealth's freedom, according to the rule of righteousness, which is God's Word. It was intended for your view above two years ago, but the disorder of the times caused me to lay it aside, with a thought never to bring it to light, etc. Likewise I hearing that Mr Peters and some others propounded this request, that the Word of God might be consulted with to find out a healing government, which I liked well and waited to see such a rule come forth, for there are good rules in the Scripture if they were obeyed and practised. Thereupon I laid aside this in silence, and said I would not make it public; but this word was like fire in my bones ever and anon, Thou shalt not bury thy talent in the earth; therefore I was stirred up to give it a resurrection, and to pick together as many of my scattered papers as I could find, and to compile them into this method, which I do here present to you, and do quiet my own spirit.

And now I have set the candle at your door, for you have power in your hand, in this other added opportunity, to act for common freedom if you will: I have no power.

It may be here are some things inserted which you may not like, yet other things you may like, therefore I pray you read it, and be as the industrious bee, suck out the honey and cast away the weeds.

Though this platform be like a piece of timber rough hewed, yet the discreet workmen may take it and frame a handsome building out of it.

It is like a poor man that comes clothed to your door in a torn country garment, who is unacquainted with the learned citizens' unsettled forms and fashions; take off the clownish language, for under that you may see beauty.

It may be you will say, 'If tithes retaken from the priests and impropriators, and copyhold services from lords of manors, how shall they be provided for again; for is it not unrighteous to take their estates from them?'

I answer, when tithes were first enacted, and lordly power drawn over the backs of the oppressed, the kings and conquerors made no scruple of conscience to take it, though the people lived in sore bondage of poverty for want of it; and can there be scruple of conscience to make restitution of this which hath been so long stolen goods? It is no scruple arising from the righteous law, but from covetousness, who goes away sorrowful to hear he must part with all to follow righteousness and peace.

But though you do take away tithes and the power of lords of manors, yet there will be no want to them, for they have the freedom of the common stock, they may send to the store-houses for what they want, and live more free than now they do; for now they are in care and vexation by servants, by casualties, by being cheated in buying and selling and many other encumbrances, but then they will be free from all, for the common store-houses is every man's riches, not any one's.

'Is it not buying and selling a righteous law?' No, it is the law of the conqueror, but not the righteous law of creation: how can that be righteous which is a cheat? For is not this a common practice, when he hath a bad horse or cow, or any bad commodity, he will send it to the market, to cheat some simple plain-hearted man or other; and when he comes home will laugh at his neighbour's hurt, and much more etc.

When mankind began to buy and sell, then did he fall from his innocence; for then they began to oppress and cozen one another of their creation birthright. As for example: if the land belong to three persons, and two of them buy and sell the earth and the third give no consent, his right is taken from him, and his posterity is engaged in a war.

When the earth was first bought and sold, many gave no consent: as when our crown lands and bishops' lands were sold, some foolish soldiers yielded, and covetous officers were active in it, to advance themselves above their brethren; but many who paid taxes and free-quarter for the purchase of it gave no consent but declared against it as an unrighteous thing, depriving posterity of their birthrights and freedoms.

Therefore this buying and selling did bring in, and still doth bring in, discontent and wars, which have plagued mankind sufficiently for so doing. And the nations of the world will never learn to beat their swords into ploughshares, and their spears into pruning hooks, and leave off warring, until this cheating device of buying and selling be cast out among the rubbish of kingly power.

'But shall not one man be richer than another?'

There is no need of that; for riches make men vain-glorious, proud, and to oppress their brethren; and are the occasion of wars.

No man can be rich, but he must be rich either by his own labours, or by the labours of other men helping him. If a man have no help from his neighbour, he shall never gather an estate of hundreds and thousands a year. If other men help him to work, then are those riches his neighbours' as well as his; for they may be the fruit of other men's labours as well as his own.

But all rich men live at ease, feeding and clothing themselves by the labours of other men, not by their own; which is their shame, and not their nobility; for it is a more blessed thing to give than to receive. But rich men receive all they have from the labourer's hand, and what they give, they give away other men's labours, not their own. Therefore they are not righteous actors in the earth.

'But shall not one man have more titles of honour than another?'

Yes. As a man goes through offices, he rises to titles of honour till he comes to the highest nobility, to be a faithful commonwealth's man in a Parliament House. Likewise he who finds out any secret in nature shall have a title of honour given him, though he be a young man. But no man shall have any title of honour till he win it by industry, or come to it by age or office-bearing. Every man that is above Sixty years of age shall have respect as a man of honour by all others that are younger, as is shewed hereafter.

'Shall every man count his neighbour's house as his own, and live together as one family?'

No. Though the earth and storehouses be common to every family, yet every family shall live apart as they do; and every man's house, wife, children and furniture for ornament of his house, or anything which he hath fetched in from the store-houses, or provided for the necessary use of his family, is all a property to that family, for the peace thereof. And if any man offer to take away a man's wife, children or furniture of his house, without his consent, or disturb the peace of his dwelling, he shall suffer punishment as an enemy to the commonwealth's government, as is mentioned in the platform following.

'Shall we have no lawyers?'

There is no need of them, for there is to be no buying and selling; neither any need to expound laws, for the bare letter of the law shall be both judge and lawyer, trying every man's actions. And seeing we shall have successive Parliaments every year, there will be rules made for every action a man can do.

But there is to be officers chosen yearly in every parish, to see the laws executed according to the letter of the laws; so that there will be no long work in trying of offences, as it is under kingly government, to get the lawyers money and to enslave the commoners to the conqueror's prerogative law or will. The sons of contention, Simeon and Levi, must not bear rule in a free commonwealth

At the first view you may say, 'This is a strange government'. But I pray judge nothing before trial. Lay this platform of commonwealth's government in one scale, and lay monarchy or kingly government in the other scale, and see which give true weight to righteous freedom and peace. There is no middle path between these two, for a man must either be a free and true commonwealth's man, or a monarchical tyrannical royalist.

If any say, 'This will bring poverty'; surely they mistake. For there will be plenty of all earthly commodities, with less labour and trouble than now it is under monarchy. There will be no want, for every man may keep as plentiful a house as he will, and never run into debt, for common stock pays for all.

If you say, 'Some will live idle': I answer, No. It will make idle persons to become workers, as is declared in the platform: there shall be neither beggar nor idle person.

If you say, 'This will make men quarrel and fight':

I answer, No. It will turn swords into ploughshares, and settle such a peace in the earth, as nations shall learn war no more. Indeed the government of kings is a breeder of wars, because men being put into the straits of poverty are moved to fight for liberty, and to take one another's estates from them, and to obtain mastery. Look into all armies, and see what they do more, but make some poor, some rich; put some into freedom, and others into bondage. And is not this a plague among mankind?

Well, I question not but what objections can be raised against this commonwealth's government, they shall find an answer in this platform following. I have been something large, because I could not contract my self into a lesser volume, having so many things to speak of.

I do not say, nor desire, that everyone shall be compelled to practise this commonwealth's government, for the spirits of some will be enemies at first, though afterwards will prove the most cordial and true friends thereunto.

Yet I desire that the commonwealth's land, which is the ancient commons and waste land, and the lands newly got in by the Army's victories out of the oppressors' hands, as parks, forests, chases and the like, may be set free to all that have lent assistance, either of person or purse, to obtain it; and to all that are willing to come in to the practice of this government and be obedient to the laws thereof. And for others who are not willing, let them stay in the way of buying and selling, which is the law of the conqueror, till they be willing.

And so I leave this in your hand, humbly prostrating myself and it before you; and remain

November 5th, 1651

Gerrard Winstanley.

To the Friendly and Unbiased Reader

Reader,

It was the apostle's advice formerly, to try all things, and to hold fast that which is best. This platform of government which I offer is the original righteousness and peace in the earth, though he hath been buried under the clods of kingly covetousness, pride and oppression a long time.

Now he begins to have his resurrection, despise it not while it is small; though thou understand it not at the first sight, yet open the door and look into the house, for thou mayst see that which will satisfy thy heart in quiet rest.

To prevent thy hasty rashness, I have given thee a short compendium of the whole.

First, thou knowest that the earth in all nations is governed by buying and selling, for all the laws of kings hath relation thereunto.

Now this platform following declares to thee the government of the earth without buying and selling, and the laws are the laws of a free and peaceable commonwealth, which casts out everything that offends; for there is no pricking briar in all this holy mountain of the righteous law or peaceable ruler.

Every family shall live apart, as now they do; every man shall enjoy his own wife, and every woman her own husband, as now they do; every trade shall be improved to more excellency than now it is; all children shall be educated, and be trained up in subjection to parents and elder people more than now they are. The earth shall be planted, and the fruits reaped and carried into store-houses, by common assistance of every family. The riches of the store-houses shall be the common stock to every family. There shall be no idle person nor beggar in the land.

And because offences may arise from the spirit of unreasonable ignorance, therefore was the law added.

For if any man abuse his neighbour by provoking words, by striking his person, by offering offence to his neighbour's Cafe or children, or to his house or furniture therein, or to live idle upon other men's labours, here are laws to punish them sharply, and officers to see those laws executed, according to the right order of commonwealth's government, for the peace of every family in the land.

This commonwealth's government unites all people in a land into one heart and mind. And it was this government which made Moses to call Abraham's seed one house of Israel, though they were many tribes and many families. And it may be said, 'Blessed is the people whose earthly government is the law of common righteousness'.

While Israel was under this commonwealth's government, they were a terror to all oppressing kings in all nations of the world; and so wig England be, if this righteous law become our governor. But when the officers of Israel began to be covetous and proud, they made a breach or, as Isaiah said, The rulers of the people caused them to err; and then the government was altered and fell into the hand of kings like other nations, and then they fled before their enemies and were scattered.

The government of kings is the government of the scribes and Pharisees, who count it no freedom unless they be lords of the earth and of their brethren. But Commonwealth's government is the government of righteousness and peace, who is no respecter of persons.

Therefore Reader, here is a trial for thy sincerity. Thou shalt have no want of food, raiment or freedom among brethren in this way propounded. See now if thou canst be content, as the Scriptures say, having food and raiment, therewith be content, and grudge not to let thy brother have the same with thee.

Dost thou pray and fast for freedom, and give God thanks again for it? Why know that God is not partial; for if thou pray, it must be for freedom to all; and if thou give thanks, it must be because freedom covers all people, for this will prove a lasting peace.

Everyone is ready to say, they fight for their country; and what they do, they do it for the good of their country. Well, let it appear now that thou hast fought and acted for thy country's freedom. But if, when thou hast power to settle freedom in thy country, thou takest the possession of the earth into thy own Particular hands, and makest thy brother work for thee as the kings did, thou has fought and acted for thyself, not for thy country; and here thy inside hypocrisy is discovered.

But here take notice that common freedom, which is the rule I would have practised and not talked on, was thy pretence;- but particular freedom to thyself was thy intent. Amend, or else thou wilt be shamed, when knowledge doth spread to cover the earth, even as the waters cover the seas And so farewell.

Chapter One

The great searching of heart in these days is to find out where true freedom lies, that the commonwealth of England might be established in peace.

Some say, 'It lies in the free use of trading, and to have all patents, licences and restraints removed'. But this is a freedom under the will of a conqueror.

Others say, 'It is true freedom to have ministers to preach, and for people to hear whom they will, without being restrained or compelled from or to any form of worship'. But this is an unsettled freedom.

Others say, 'It is true freedom to have community with all women, and to have liberty to satisfy their lusts and greedy appetites'. But this is the freedom of wanton unreasonable beasts, and tends to destruction.

Others say, 'It is true freedom that the elder brother shall be landlord of the earth, and the younger brother a servant'. And this is but a half freedom, and begets murmurings, wars and quarrels.

All these and such like are freedoms: but they lead to bondage, and are not the true foundation-freedom which settles a commonwealth in peace.

True commonwealth's freedom lies in the free enjoyment of the earth.

True freedom lies where a man receives his nourishment and preservation, and that is in the use of the earth. For as man is compounded of the four materials of the creation, fire, water, earth and air; so is he preserved by the compounded bodies of these four, which are the fruits of the earth; and he cannot live without them. For take away the free use of these and the body languishes, the spirit is brought into bondage and at length departs, and ceaseth his motional action in the body.

All that a man labours for, saith Solomon, is this, That he may enjoy the free use of the earth, with the fruits thereof. Eccles. 2.24.

Do not the ministers preach for maintenance in the earth? the lawyers plead causes to get the possessions of the earth? Doth not the soldier fight for the earth? And doth not the landlord require rent, that he may live in the fulness of the earth by the labour of his tenants?

And so, from the thief upon the highway to the king who sits upon the throne, do not everyone strive, either by force of arms or secret cheats, to get the possessions of the earth one from another, because they see their freedom lies in plenty, and their bondage lies in poverty?

Surely then, oppressing lords of manors, exacting landlords and tithe-takers, may as well say their brethren shall not breathe in the air, nor enjoy warmth in their bodies, nor have the moist waters to fall upon them in showers, unless they will pay them rent for it: as to say their brethren shall not work upon earth, nor eat the fruits thereof, unless they will hire that liberty of them. For he that takes upon him to restrain his brother from the liberty of the one, may upon the same ground restrain him from the liberty of all four, viz. fire, water, earth and air,

A man had better to have had no body than to have no food for it; therefore this restraining of the earth from brethren by brethren is oppression and bondage; but the free enjoyment thereof is true freedom.

I speak now in relation between the oppressor and the oppressed; the inward bondages I meddle not with in this place, though I am assured that, if it be rightly searched into, the inward bondages of the mind, as covetousness, pride, hypocrisy, envy, sorrow, fears, desperation and madness, are all occasioned by the outward bondage that one sort of people lay upon another.

And thus far natural experience makes it good, that true freedom lies in the free enjoyment of the earth.

If we look into the old Scriptures,

We find that when Israel had conquered the nations he took possession of the enemies' land, and divided it by lot among the tribes, counting the enjoyment of the earth their perfect freedom.

In the beginning of their wars they first sent spies to view the land of Canaan (Numb. 13.23 to 33), for the enjoyment of that was the freedom they aimed at, for being so long in the barren wilderness, and children multiplying upon them, they wanted land to live upon, Deut. 1.28.

And when the spies returned and shewed them the fruits of the land, and had declared what a fruitful land it was, they were encouraged and restless till they were come thither; and when they heard bad tidings of the land, their hearts fell and they were discouraged.

And when the spirit of wisdom, courage and providence in them had subdued those giants, and had given the house of Israel the land of Canaan, the rulers and chief officers of Israel's army did not divide the land among themselves; but, being faithful-spirited men, they forthwith divided the land by lot, to every tribe his portion without exception.

And when Israel entreated the King of Sihon to suffer him to pass through his land, he would not suffer him, but gathered all his people together and fought with Israel; and the Lord gave Sihon into Israel's hand: and he took possession of his land.

So that we see by Scripture proof likewise, the land is that which everyone place their freedom in.

If we look into the practice of kings and conquerors,

Since the Scriptures of Moses were writ, we find they placed their freedom in the enjoyment of the free use of the earth.

When William Duke of Normandy had conquered England, he took possession of the earth for his freedom and disposed of our English ground to his friends as he pleased, and made the conquered English his servants, to plant the earth for him and his friends.

And all kings, from his time to King Charles, were successors of that conquest; and all laws were made to confirm that conquest.

For there are his old laws and statutes yet to be read, that do shew how he allowed the conquered English but three pence and four pence a day for their work, to buy them bread of their task-masters; but the freedom of the earth he and his friends kept in their own hands.

And as kings, so the old gentry and the new gentry likewise, walking in the same steps, are but the successors of the Norman victory.

But are not the Normans and their power conquered by the commoners of England? And why then should we not recover the freedom of our land again, from under that yoke and power?

Then further, the Norman conqueror made laws whereby this English earth should be governed, and appointed two national officers to see those laws performed.

The first officer was the lawyer; and his work is conversant about nothing but the disposing of the earth, and all courts of judicature and suits of law is about the ordering of the earth, according to his law made by him and his party.

The next officer was the national clergy; and their work was to persuade the multitude of people to let William the Conqueror alone with a quiet possession and government of the earth, and to call it his and not theirs, and so not to rebel against him.

And they were to tell the people that if they would acknowledge William Duke of Normandy and his successors to be their lord, king and ruler, and would be obedient to his government: then they should live in the haven, that is, in peace; and they should quietly enjoy their land which they rented, their houses and fruits of their labours without disturbance.

But if they would not acknowledge him to be their lord, king and ruler, nor submit to his government, then they should be cast into hell; that is, into the sorrows of prisons, poverty, whips and death: and their houses and riches should be taken from them, etc.

And this was a true prophetical and experimental doctrine. For do we not see that the laws of a king, while a king, had the power of life and death in them? And he who fell under the power of this lord [2] must pay the uttermost farthing before he was released.

And for their pains for thus preaching, the king established by his laws that they should have the tenth of the increase of all profits from the earth (I Sam. 8.15), placing their freedom where he placed his own, and that is in the use of the earth brought into their hands by the labours of the enslaved men.

But in after times, when this national ministry appeared to the people to be but hirelings, and as the people grew in knowledge, they discovered their hypocrisy more and more, as they do in these days: then this clergy (the spirit of the old Pharisees) began to divine and to deceive the people by a shew of holiness or spiritual doctrine, as they call it, difficult to be understood by any but themselves; persuading the people to believe or fancy that true freedom lay in hearing them preach, and to enjoy that heaven which, they say, every man who believes their doctrine shall enjoy after he is dead: and so tell us of a heaven and hell after death, which neither they nor we know what will be. So that the whole world is at a loss in the true knowledge thereof, as Solomon said, Who shall bring him to see what shall be after he is dead? Eccles. 3.22 and 6.11.

The former hell of prisons, whips and gallows they preached to keep the people in subjection to the king; but by this divined hell after death they preach to keep both king and people in awe to them, to uphold their trade of tithes and new-raised maintenance. And so having blinded both king and people they become the god that rules. This subtle divining spirit is the Whore that sits upon many waters; this is Nahash the Ammonite, that would not make peace with Israel, unless Israel would suffer him to put out their right eyes and to see by his, I Sam. I I.2.

For so long as the people call that a truth which they call a truth, and believe what they preach, and are willing to let the clergy be the keepers of their eyes and knowledge (that is as much as Nahash did, put out their eyes to see by theirs); then all is well, and they tell the people they shall go to heaven.

But if the eyes of the people begin to open, and they seek to find knowledge in their own hearts and to question the ministers' doctrine, and become like unto wise-hearted Thomas, to believe nothing but what they see reason for:

Then do the minsters prepare war against that man or men, and will make no covenant of peace with him till they consent to have their right eyes put out, that is, to have their reason blinded, so as to believe every doctrine they preach and never question any thing, saying, 'The doctrine of faith must not be tried by reason.' No, for if it be, their mystery of iniquity will be discovered, and they would lose their tithes.

Therefore no marvel though the national clergy of England and Scotland, who are the tithing priests and lords of blinded men's spirits, stuck so close to their master the King and to his monarchical oppressing government; for say they, 'If the people must not work for us and give us tithes, but we must work for ourselves as they do, our freedom is lost'. Aye, but this is but the cry of an Egyptian task-master, who counts other men's freedom his bondage.

Now if the earth could be enjoyed in such a manner as everyone might have provision, as it may by this platform I have offered, then will the peace of the commonwealth be preserved, and men need not act so hypocritically as the clergy do, and others likewise, to get a living. But when some shall enjoy great possessions, and others who have done as much or more for to purchase freedom shall have none at all, and be made slaves to their brethren, this begets offences.

The glory of Israel's commonwealth is this:

They had no beggar among them.

As you read, when they had conquered the Canaanites and won that land by the purchase of the blood and labour, and by a joint assistance throughout the whole tribes of Israel; the officers and leaders of the people did not sell the land again to the remainder of their enemies, nor buy and sell it among themselves, and so by cheating the people set up a new oppression upon a new account. Neither did they fall a-parting the land before the crowning victory was gotten: but they forbore the disposing of the land till the war was over, and all the tribes stuck close together till all the fighting work was done.

And when they saw the enemies' heart was broke, and that now they were the masters of the field, then they quietly took possession of the land as a free reward for all their hazards and labour.

The officers and leaders were careful to keep promise and engagements to the people, and there was no treachery found in them, as to enrich themselves with the commonwealth's land, and to deprive others of the price of their blood and free-quarter and taxes.

But they made canon with all the crown lands therein, and all other forfeited lands which was gotten by a joint assistance of person and purse of all the tribes. The Scriptures say, they made this canon land a common treasury of livelihood to the whole commonwealth of Israel, and so disposed of it as they made provision for every tribe and for every family in a tribe, nay for every particular man in a family; everyone had enough, no man was in want, there was no beggary among them.

They did not divide this land only to particular men who went out to war, but they who stayed at home had an equal share; they did not make one brother a lord of manor and landlord, and other brothers to be servants to them. But seeing the enemies were beaten not by the counsellors only, not by the leaders of the army only, but by the common soldiers also; and not only by them, but by the labourers who stayed at home to provide victuals and free-quarter: therefore did the counsellors and chief officers of the army agree to make provision for everyone that assisted, either by person or purse; and this was pure righteousness.

And to those families in a tribe which had many persons in it, to them they allotted more land; and to those families which had less number of persons, they allotted less land. So that not only the tribes in general but every family and person in a tribe, younger brother as well as elder brother, he who wrought at home to provide food as well as he that went to war, all had sufficient, there was no want, the oppression of beggary was not known among them. All burdens were taken off, and Israel in all his tribes and families was made a free commonwealth in power, as well as in name, I Sam. 30.24, Josh. 16, 17 and 18 Chapters.

And thus the land was divided, and the whole land was the common stock, everyone had a brotherly freedom therein. For the freedom of the one was the freedom of the other, there was no difference in that, they were men of true, faithful and public spirits not false-hearted.

And so likewise When Esther prevailed with Ring Ahasuerus for freedom, she did not seek her own freedom and interest, but the freedom of all her kindred and friends; for common freedom was that which men of righteous spirits always sought after.

All that I shall say is this, O that those who pretend to set up a gospel-commonwealth in England, Scotland and Ireland would not be worse than Moses, but rather exceed Moses, knowing that if this our English commonwealth's government carry perfect freedom in his hand, then shall the law go forth from England to all the nations of the world.

This foundation being laid from the example of Israel's commonwealth and testimony of God's Word, I shall proceed how the earth shall be governed for the peace of a commonwealth. But by the way, to prevent mistake, I shall insert

A short declaration to take off Prejudice:

Some, hearing of this common freedom, think there must be a community of all the fruits of the earth whether they work or no, therefore strive to live idle upon other men's labours.

Others, through the same unreasonable beastly ignorance, think there must be a community of all men and women for copulation, and so strive to live a bestial life.

Others think there will be no law, but that everything will run into confusion for want-of government; but this platform proves the contrary.

Therefore, because that transgression doth and may arise from ignorant and rude fancy in man, is the law added.

That which true righteousness in my judgment calls community is this, to have the earth set free from all kingly bondage of lords of manors and oppressing landlords, which came in by conquest as a thief takes a true man's purse upon the highway, being stronger than he.

And that neither the earth, nor any fruits thereof, should be bought or sold by the inhabitants one among another, which is slavery the kingly conquerors have brought in; therefore he set his stamp upon silver, that everyone should buy and sell in his name.

And though this be, yet shall not men live idle; for the earth shall be planted and reaped, and the fruits carried into barns and store-houses by the assistance of every family, according as is shewed hereafter in order.

Every man shall be brought up in trades and labours, and all trades shall be maintained with more improvement, to the enriching of the commonwealth, more than now they be under kingly power.

Every tradesman shall fetch materials, as leather, wool, flax, corn and the like, from the public store-houses, to work upon without buying and selling; and when particular works are made, as cloth, shoes, hats and the like, the tradesmen shall bring these particular works to particular shops, as it is now in practice, without buying and selling. And every family as they want such things as they cannot make, they shall go to these shops and fetch without money, even as now they fetch with money, as hereafter is shewed how in order.

If any say, 'This will nurse idleness'; I answer, this platform proves the contrary, for idle persons and beggars will be made to work.

If any say, 'This will make some men to take goods from others by violence and call it theirs, because the earth and fruits are a common stock'; I answer, the laws or rules following prevents that ignorance. For though the store-houses and public shops be commonly furnished by every family's assistance, and for every family's use, as is shewed hereafter how: yet every man's house is proper to himself, and all the furniture therein, and provision which he hath fetched from the store-houses is proper to himself; every man's wife and every woman's husband proper to themselves, and so are their children at their dispose till they come to age.

And if any other man endeavour to take away his house, furniture, food, wife or children, saying everything is common, and so abusing the law of peace, such a one is a transgressor, and shall suffer punishment, as by the government and laws following is expressed.

For though the public store-houses be a common treasury, yet every man's particular dwelling is not common but by his consent, and the commonwealth's laws are to preserve a man's peace in his person and in his private dwelling, against the rudeness and ignorance that may arise in mankind.

If any man do force or abuse women in folly, pleading community, the laws following do punish such ignorant and unrational practice; for the laws of a commonwealth are laws of moderate diligence and purity of manners.

Therefore I desire a patient reading of what hereafter follows; and when you have heard the extent of commonwealth's government or freedom, then weigh it in the balance with kingly government or bondage; and see whether [i.e. which] brings most peace to the land, and establish that for government.

For you must either establish commonwealth's freedom in power, making provision for everyone's peace, which is righteousness; or else you must set up monarchy again.

Monarchy is twofold; either for one king to rule, or for many to rule by kingly principles; for the king's power lies in his laws, not in the name. And if either one king rule, or many rule by king's principles, much murmuring, grudges, troubles and quarrels may and will arise among the oppressed people upon every gained opportunity.

But if common freedom be found out and ease the oppressed, it prevents murmurings and quarrels, and establishes universal peace in the earth.

Therefore seeing the power of government is in the hands of such as have professed to the world a godly righteousness, more purely than that of oppressing kings, without doubt their faithfulness and wisdom is required to be manifested in action as well as in words.

But if they who profess more righteousness and freedom in words than the kings' government was, and yet can find out no government to ease the people but must establish the kings' old laws though they give it a new name; I will leave the sentence, worthy such a profession and such a people, to be given by the heart of every rational man. And so I shall proceed how the earth should be governed for the peace of a commonwealth.

Chapter Two:

What is Government in general?

Government is a wise and free ordering of the earth and the manners of mankind by observation of particular laws or rules, so that all the inhabitants may live peaceably in plenty and freedom in the land where they are born and bred.

In the government of a land there are three parts, viz. laws, fit officers and a faithful execution of those laws.

First, there must be suitable laws for every occasion, and almost for every action that men do; for one law cannot serve in all seasons, but every season and every action have their particular laws attending thereupon for the preservation of right order. As for example,

There is a time to plough, and the laws of right understanding attends upon that work; and there is a time to reap the fruits of the earth, and the laws of right observation attending thereupon.

So that true government is a right ordering of all actions, giving to every action and thing its due weight and measure, and this prevents confusion. As Solomon speaks, There is a time for all things; a time to make promises and engagements and a time to see them performed; a right order in times of war, and a right order in times of peace; every season and time having its law or rule suitable; and this makes a healthful government, because it preserves peace in a right order.

Secondly, there must be fit officers, whose spirits are so humble, wise and free from covetousness, as they can make the established laws of the land their will; and not through pride and vain-glory make their wills to rule above the rules of freedom, pleading prerogative.

For when the right ordered laws do rule, the government is healthful; but when the will of officers rule above law, that government is diseased with a mortal disease.

Thirdly, there must be a faithful execution of those laws; and herein lies the very life of government. For a right order in government lies not in the will of officers without laws, nor in laws without officers, nor in neither of them without execution. But when these three go hand in hand the government is healthful; but if any one of these be wanting the government is diseased.

There is a twofold government, a kingly government and a commonwealth's government.

What is kingly government or monarchy?

Kingly government governs the earth by that cheating art of buying and selling, and thereby becomes a man of contention, his hand is against every man, and every man's hand against him; and take this government at the best, it is a diseased government, and the very city Babylon, full of confusion. And if it had not a club law to support it, there would be no order in it, because it is the covetous and proud will of a conqueror, enslaving a conquered people.

This kingly government is he who beats pruning hooks and ploughs into spears, guns, swords and instruments of war, that he might take his younger brother's creation birthright from him, calling the earth his and not his brother's, unless his brother will hire the earth of him, so that he may live idle and at ease by his brother's labours.

Indeed this government may well be called the government of highwaymen, who hath stolen the earth from the younger brethren by force, and holds it from them by force. He sheds blood not to free the people from oppression, but that he may be king and ruler over an oppressed people.

The situation of this monarchical government...

Lies in the will of kings, alias conquerors, setting up lords of manors, exacting landlords, tithing priests and covetous lawyers, with all those pricking briars attending thereupon, to be task-masters to oppress the people, lest they should rise up in riches and power to disthrone him, and so to share the earth with him, redeeming their own creation rights again, which this kingly government withholds from mankind in all nations. For he is the great Man of Sin who is now revealed, who sits in the temple of God, ruling above all that is called God, and both by force and cheating policy takes the people's freedoms from them, Exod. 1.8, 2 Thes. 2.8,9.

This kingly government is he that makes the elder brethren freemen in the earth, and the younger brethren slaves in the earth, before they have lost their freedom by transgression to the law.

Nay, he makes one brother a lord and another a servant while they are in their mother's womb, before they have done either good or evil. This is the mighty ruler that hath made the election and rejection of brethren from their birth to their death, or frown eternity to eternity.

He calls himself the Lord God of the whole creation, for he makes one brother to pay rent to another brother for the use of the water, earth and air, or else he will not suffer him by his laws and lawyers to live above ground, but in beggary; and yet he will be called righteous.

And whereas the Scriptures say that the creator of all things (God) is no respecter of persons, yet this kingly power doth nothing else but respect persons, preferring the rich and the proud; therefore he denies the Scriptures and the true God of righteousness, though he pray and preach of the Scriptures, and keep fasts and thanksgiving-days to God, to be a cloak to hide his oppression from the people, whereby he shews himself to be the great Antichrist and mystery of iniquity, that makes war with Christ and his saints under pretence of owning him.

The great law-giver of this kingly government...

Is covetousness ruling in the heart of mankind, making one brother to covet a full possession of the earth and a lordly rule over another brother, which he will have or else he will enslave or kill his brother;

for this is Cain who killed Abel: and because of this, he is called the great red dragon, the god of this world, the oppressor, under which the whole creation hath groaned a long time, waiting to be delivered from him.

The rise of kingly government is twofold:

First, by a politic wit, in drawing the people out of common freedom into a way of common bondage; for so long as the earth is a common treasury to all men, kingly covetousness can never reign as king. Therefore his first device was to put the people to buy and sell the earth and the fruits one to another; for this would beget discontents and muddy the waters.

And when this spirit of monarchy hath drawn the people into the way of buying and selling, and the people begin to vex one another, then began his opportunity to reign.

For in that man wherein this kingly spirit seats himself, he tells the people that are wronged, 'Well, I'll ease you, and I'll set things to rights'. And then he went about to establish buying and selling by law, whereby the people had some ease for a time, but the cunning Machiavellian spirit got strength thereby to settle himself king in the earth.

For after some time the people through ignorance began to multiply suits of law one against another, and to quarrel and fight. Now saith this subtle spirit, 'Come follow me' to one sort of people that are oppressed, 'and stick to me, and we will fight with those who wrong you; and if we conquer them, then we will govern the earth as we please, and they shall be our servants, and we will make them work for us'.

Thereupon one sort of people followed one head, and another sort of people followed another head, and so wars began in the earth, and mankind fell a-fighting, one part conquering and enslaving another. And now man is fallen from his innocence, and from the glory of the spirit of common freedom, love and peace, into enmity; everyone striving to be king one over another; everyone striving to be a landlord of the earth, and to make his brother his servant to work for him.

But still here is disorder, therefore this subtle spirit of darkness goes further and tells the people, 'You must make one man king over you all, and let him make laws, and let everyone be obedient thereunto'. And when the people consented thereunto, they gave away their freedom, and they set up oppression over themselves.

And this was the rise of kingly power: first by policy, drawing the people from a common enjoyment of the earth to the crafty art of buying and selling; secondly, to advance himself by the power of the sword, when that art of buying and selling had made them quarrel among themselves.

So that this spirit of monarchy it is the spirit of subtlety and covetousness, filling the heart of mankind with enmity and ignorance, pride and vain-glory, because the strong destroys the weak; and so one Scripture calls this the power and government of the Beast, another Scripture calls it the god of this world or the devil. For indeed the monarchical spirit is the power of darkness, for it is the great thick cloud that hath hid the light of the sun of righteousness from shining in his full strength a long time.

And though this kingly spirit doth call buying and selling a righteous thing, thereby to put the simple younger brother upon it, yet he will destroy it as he pleaseth, by patents, licences or monopolizing.

Or else he will at his pleasure take away the riches which his younger brother hath got by trading, and so still lift up himself above his brother.

And as he rise to the throne by the crafty art of buying and selling and by the sword, so he is maintained upon the throne by the same means.

And the people now see that kingly power is the oppressor, and the maintainers thereof are called oppressors by the ancient writers of the Bible.

This kingly power is the old heaven and the old earth that must pass away, wherein unrighteousness, oppression and partiality dwells.

For indeed we never read that the people began to complain of oppression till kingly government rose up, which is the power of covetousness and pride; and which Samuel sets forth to be a plague and a curse upon the people in the first rise of it.

He will take your sons and your daughters to be his servants and to run before his chariots, to plant his ground and to reap his harvest. He will take your fields, your vineyards and olive-yards, even the best of them, and give to his servants as pleaseth him. He will take the tenth of your seed and of your vineyards and give to his officers or ministers. I Sam. 8.

And this was that god who appointed the people to pay tithes to the clergy.

And many other oppressions did the kingly government bring upon the people, as you may read at large in Samuel.

Read I Sam. 8. from Vers. 10. to 19.

The winter's past, the spring time now appears,
Begone thou kingly tyrant, with all thy Cavaliers.
Thy day is past, and sure thou dost appear
To be the bond-man's son, and not the free-born heir.
Matt. 15. 13

What is commonwealth's government?

Commonwealth's government governs the earth without buying and selling; and thereby becomes a man of peace, and the restorer of ancient peace and freedom. He makes provision for the oppressed, the weak and the simple, as well as for the rich, the wise and the strong. He beats swords and spears into pruning hooks and ploughs; he makes both elder and younger brother freemen in the earth. Micah 4.3, 4, Isai. 33.1. and 65.17 to 25.

All slaveries and oppressions which have been brought upon mankind by kings, lords of manors, lawyers and landlords and the divining clergy, are all cast out again by this government, if it be right in power as well as in name.

For this government is the true restorer of all long-lost freedoms, and so becomes the joy of all nations, and the blessing of the whole earth:

for this takes off the kingly curse, and makes Jerusalem a praise in the earth. Therefore all you who profess religion and spiritual things, now look to it, and see what spirit you do profess, for your profession is brought to trial.

If once commonwealth's government be set upon the throne, then no tyranny or oppression can look him in the face and live.

For where oppression lies upon brethren by brethren, that is no commonwealth's government, but the kingly government still; and the mystery of iniquity hath taken that peace-maker's name to be a cloak to hide his subtle covetousness, pride and oppression under.

O England, England, wouldst thou have thy government sound and healthful? Then cast about and see and search diligently to find out all those burdens that came in by kings, and remove them; and then will thy commonwealth's government arise from under the clods, under which as yet it is buried and covered with deformity.

If true commonwealth's freedom lie in the free enjoyment of the earth, as it doth, then whatsoever law or custom doth deprive brethren of their freedom in the earth, it is to be cast out as unsavory salt.

The situation of commonwealth's government...

Is within the laws of common freedom, whereby there is a provision for livelihood in the earth both for elder and younger brother; and not the one enslaving the other, but both living in plenty and freedom.

The officers, laws and customs hereafter mentioned, or such like, according to such a method, may be the foundation and pillars of commonwealth's government.

This government depends not upon the will of any particular man or men; for it is seated in the spirit of mankind, and it is called the light, or son of righteousness and peace. The tyrants in all ages have made use of this man's name while he hath lain buried, to cover their cheating mystery of iniquity: for if common freedom were not pretended, the commoners of a land would never dance after the pipe of self-seeking wits.

This commonwealth's government may well be called the ancient of days; for it was before any other oppressing government crept in.

It is the moderator of all oppression; and so is like Moses and Joseph in Pharaoh's court, and in time will be the restorer of long lost freedoms to the creation, and delights to plant righteousness over the face of the whole earth.

The great lawgiver in commonwealth's government…

Is the spirit of universal righteousness dwelling in mankind, now rising up to teach everyone to do to another as he would have another do to him, and is no respecter of persons: and this spirit hath been killed in the Pharisaical kingly spirit of self-love, and been buried in the dunghill of that enmity for many years past.

And if these be the days of his resurrection to power, as we may hope, because the name of commonwealth is risen and established in England by a law, then we or our posterity shall see comfortable effects.

In that nation where this commonwealth's government shall be first established, there shall be abundance of peace and plenty, and all nations of the earth shall come flocking thither to see his beauty, and to learn the ways thereof; and the law shall go forth from that Sion, and that Word of the Lord from that Jerusalem, which shall govern the whole earth. Micah 4.1, 2.

There shall be no tyrant kings, lords of manors, tithing priests, oppressing lawyers, exacting landlords, nor any such like pricking briar in all this holy mountain of the Lord God our righteousness and peace; for the righteous law shall be the rule for everyone, and the judge of all men's actions.

David desired rather to be a door-keeper in this house of God, or commonwealth's government, than to live in the tents of wickedness, which was the kingly oppressing courts.

If any go about to build up commonwealth's government upon kingly principles, they will both shame and lose themselves; for there is a plain difference between the two governments.

And if you do not run in the right channel of freedom, you must, nay you will, as you do, face about and turn back again to Egyptian monarchy: and so your names in the days of posterity shall stink and be blasted with abhorred infamy for your unfaithfulness to common freedom; and the evil effects will be sharp upon the backs of posterity.

Therefore seeing England is declared to be a free commonwealth, and the name thereof established by a law; surely then the greatest work is now to be done, and that is to escape all kingly cheats in setting up a commonwealth's government, that the power and the name may agree together; so that all the inhabitants may live in peace, plenty and freedom, otherwise we shall shew our government to be gone no further but to the half day of the Beast, or to the dividing of time, of which there must be an overturn. Dan. 7.25, Rev. 12.14.

For oppression was always the occasion why the spirit of freedom in the people desired change of government.

When Samuel's sons took bribes and grew rich upon the common purse, and forgot to relieve the oppressed, that made the people forsake the government by judges, and to desire a kingly government. I Sam. 8.34.

And the oppressions of the kingly government have made this age of the world to desire a commonwealth's government and the removal of the kings; for the spirit of light in man loves freedom and hates bondage.

And because the spirit in mankind is various within itself, for some are wise, some are foolish, some idle, some laborious, some rash, some mild, some loving and free to others, some envious and covetous, some of an inclination to do as they would have others do to them, but others seek to save themselves and to live in fulness, though others perish for want:

Therefore because of this was the law added, which was to be a rule and judge for all men's actions, to preserve common peace and freedom; and Paul writ, The law was added because of transgression, one against another.

The haven gates are now set ope for English man to enter: The freedoms of the earth's his due, if he will make adventure.

Chapter Three:

Where began the first original of Government in the Earth among Mankind?

The original root of magistracy is common preservation, and it rose up first in a private family: for suppose there were but one family in the world, as is conceived, father Adam's family, wherein were many persons:

Therein Adam was the first governor or officer in the earth, because as he was the first father, so he was the most wise in contriving and the most strong for labour, and so the fittest to be the chief governor. For this is the golden rule,

Let the wise help the foolish, and let the strong help the weak. Psa. 35.10, Rom. 15. 1, 2.

But some may say here that Adam was under no law, but his will was a law to him and his household; therefore, from the root from whence magistracy first rose, it is clear that officers are to be under no law but their own wills, and the people are to be subject thereunto.[4] I answer:

The law of necessity, that the earth should be planted for the common preservation and peace of his household, was the righteous rule and law to Adam, and this law was so clearly written in the hearts of his people that they all consented quietly to any counsel he gave them for that end.

Therefore not Adam's will only, but the will of his people likewise, and the law of common preservation, peace and freedom, was the righteous law that governed both Adam and his household.

But yet observe, that from the father in a family was the first rise of magisterial government, because children wanting experience of their own preservation, therefore such as are experienced are to propound the law of government to them: and therefore from Adam to this day, the law of common preservation is the rule and foundation of true magistracy: and it is the work of all magistrates to help the weak and the foolish.

There are two roots from whence laws do spring:

The first root you see is common preservation, when there is a principle in everyone to seek the good of others as himself, without respecting persons: and this is the root of the tree magistracy, and the law of righteousness and peace: and all particular laws found out by experience, necessary to be practised for common preservation, are the boughs and branches of that tree.

And because, among the variety of mankind, ignorance may grow up; therefore this original law is written in the heart of every man, to be his guide or leader: so that if an officer be blinded by covetousness and pride, and that ignorance rule in him, yet an inferior man may tell him where he goes astray; for common preservation and peace is the foundation rule of all government. And therefore if any will preach or practise fundamental truths or doctrine, here you may see where the foundation thereof lies.

The second root is self-preservation: when particular officers seek their own preservation, ease; honour, riches and freedom in the earth, and do respect persons that are in power and riches with them and regard not the peace, freedom and preservation of the weak and foolish among brethren.

And this is the root of the tree tyranny, and the law of unrighteousness; and all particular kingly laws found out by covetous policy to enslave one brother to another, whereby bondage, tears, sorrows and poverty are brought upon many men, are all but the boughs and branches of that tree, tyranny; and such officers as these are fallen from true magistracy, and are no members thereof, but the members of tyranny, who is the devil and Satan.

And indeed this tyranny is the cause of all wars and troubles, and of the removal of the government of the earth oust of one hand into another, so often as it is, in all nations.

For if magistrates had a care to cherish the peace and liberties of the common people, and see them set free from oppression, they might sit in the chair of government and never be disturbed.

But when their sitting is altogether to advance their own interest, and to forget the afflictions of Joseph or their brethren that are under bondage: this is a forerunner of their own downfall, and oftentime proves the plague to the whole land.

Therefore the work of all true magistrates is to maintain the common law, which is the root of right government and preservation and peace to everyone; and to cast out all self-ended principles and interests, which is tyranny and oppression, and which breaks common peace.

For surely the disorderly actings of officers break the peace of the commonwealth more than any men whatsoever.

All officers in a true magistracy of a commonwealth are to be chosen officers.

In the first family, which is the foundation from whence all families sprang, there was the father; he is the first link of the chain magistracy. The necessity of the children that sprang from him doth say,

'Father, do thou teach us how to plant the earth, that we may live, and we will obey'. By this choice they make him not only a father, but a master and ruler. And out of this root springs up all magistrates and officers, to see the law executed and to preserve peace in the earth, by seeing that right government is observed.

For here take notice, that though the children might not speak, yet their weakness and simplicity did speak and chose their father to be their overseer.

So that he who is a true commonwealth's officer is not to step into the place of magistracy by policy or violent force, as all kings and conquerors do; and so become oppressing tyrants, by promoting their self-ended interests or Machiavellian cheats, that they may live in plenty and rule as lords over their brethren.

But a true commonwealth's officer is to be a chosen one, by them who are in necessity and who judge him fit for that work.

And thus a father in a family is a commonwealth's officer, because the necessity of the young children chose him by a joint consent, and not otherwise.

Secondly, in a bigger family called a parish, the body of the people are confused and disordered, because some are wise, some foolish, some subtle and cunning to deceive, others plain-hearted, some strong, some weak, some rash, angry, some mild and quiet-spirited. By reason whereof offences do arise among brethren, and their common peace is broken.

Therefore as necessity hath added a law to limit men's manners, because of transgressions one against another,

So likewise doth the necessity of common peace move the whole body of the parish to choose two, three or more, within that circuit, to be their overseers, to cause the unruly ones, for whom only the law was added, to be subject to the law or rule, that so peace may be preserved among them in the planting of the earth, reaping the fruits, and quiet enjoyment.

Thirdly, in every county, shire or land, wherein the families are increased to a larger commonwealth, the necessity of the people moves them still to choose more overseers and officers to preserve common peace.

And when the people have chosen all officers, to preserve a right order in government of [the] earth among them, then doth the same necessity of common peace move the people to say to their overseers and officers:

'Do you see our laws observed for our preservation and peace, and we will assist and protect you.' And this word 'assist' and 'protect' implies:

The rising up of the people by force of arms to defend their laws and officers against any invasion, rebellion or resistance, yea to beat down the turbulence of any foolish or self-ended spirit that endeavours to break their common peace.

So that all true officers are chosen officers, and when they act to satisfy the necessity of them who chose them, then they are faithful and righteous servants to that commonwealth, and then there is a rejoicing in the city.

But when officers do take the possessions of the earth into their own hands, lifting themselves up thereby to be lords over their masters, the people who chose them, and will not suffer the people to plant the earth and reap the fruits for their livelihood, unless they will hire the land of them or work for day-wages for them, that they may live in ease and plenty and not work:

These officers are fallen from true magistracy of a commonwealth, and they do not act righteously; and because of this, sorrows and tears, poverty and bondages, are known among mankind; and now that city mourns.

And surely if it be carefully looked into, the necessity of the people never chose such officers, but they were either voluntary soldiers or officers chosen by them who ran before they were called; and so by policy and force they sat down in the chair of government, strengthening one sort of people to take the free use of the earth from another sort; and these are sons of bondage, and they act in darkness: by reason whereof the prophet Isaiah cries out, Darkness hath covered the earth, and thick darkness the people; for the leaders of the people have caused them to err: I fear so, O England, etc.

All officers in a commonwealth are to be chosen new ones every year.

When public officers remain long in place of judicature, they will degenerate from the bounds of humility, honesty and tender care of brethren, in regard the heart of man is so subject to be overspread with the clouds of covetousness, pride and vain-glory: for though at the first entrance into places of rule they be of public spirits, seeking the freedom of others as their own; yet continuing long in such a place where honours and greatness is coming in, they become selfish, seeking themselves and not common freedom; as experience proves it true in these days, according to this common proverb,

Great offices in a land and army have changed the disposition of many sweet-spirited men.

And nature tells us that if water stand long, it corrupts; whereas running water keeps sweet and is fit for common use.

Therefore as the necessity of common preservation moves the people to frame a law and to choose officers to see the law obeyed, that they may live in peace:

So doth the same necessity bid the people, and cries aloud in the ears and eyes of England to choose new officers and to remove the old ones, and to choose state-officers every year; and that for these reasons:

First, to prevent their own evils; for when pride and fulness take hold of an officer, his eyes are so blinded therewith that he forgets he is a servant to the commonwealth, and strives to lift up himself high above his brethren, and oftentimes his fall proves very great: witness the fall of oppressing kings, bishops and other state officers.

Secondly, to prevent the creeping in of oppression into the commonwealth again: for when officers grow proud and full, they will maintain their greatness, though it be in the poverty, ruin and hardship of their brethren: witness the practice of kings and their laws, that have crushed the commoners of England a long time.

And have we not experience in these days that some officers of the commonwealth are grown so mossy for want of removing that they will hardly speak to an old acquaintance, if he be an inferior man, though they were very familiar before these wars began? Etc.

And what hath occasioned this distance among friends and brethren but long continuance in places of honour, greatness and riches?

Thirdly, let officers be chosen new every year in love to our posterity; for if burdens and oppressions should grow up in our laws and in our officers for want of removing, as moss and weeds grow in some land for want of stirring, surely it will be a foundation of misery, not easily to be removed by our posterity; and then will they curse the time that ever we their fore-fathers had opportunities to set things to rights for their ease, and would not do it.

Fourthly, to remove officers of state every year will make them truly faithful, knowing that others are coming after who will look into their ways; and if they do not do things justly, they must be ashamed when the next officers succeed. And when officers deal faithfully in the government of the commonwealth, they will not be unwilling to remove. The peace of London is much preserved by removing their officers yearly.

Fifthly, it is good to remove officers every year, that whereas many have their portions to obey, so many may have their turns to rule; and this will encourage all men to advance righteousness and good manners in hopes of honour; but when money and riches bears all the sway in the rulers' hearts, there is nothing but tyranny in such ways.

Sixthly, the commonwealth hereby will be furnished with able and experienced men, fit to govern, which will mightily advance the honour and peace of our land, occasion the more watchful care in the education of children, and in time will make our commonwealth of England the lily among the nations of the earth.

Who are fit to choose, and fit to be chosen, officers in a commonwealth?

All uncivil livers, as drunkards, quarrellers, fearful ignorant men, who dare not speak truth lest they anger other men; likewise all who are wholly given to pleasure and sports, or men who are full of talk; all these are empty of substance, and cannot be experienced men, therefore not fit to be chosen officers in a commonwealth; yet they may have a voice in the choosing.

Secondly, all those who are interested in the monarchical power and government ought - neither to choose nor be chosen officers to manage commonwealth's affairs, for these cannot be friends to common freedom. And these are of two sorts:

First, such as have either lent money to maintain the King's army, or in that army have been soldiers to fight against the recovering of common freedom; these are neither to choose nor be chosen officers in the commonwealth as yet, for they have lost their freedom; yet I do not say that they should be made servants, as the conquered usually are made servants, for they are our brethren, and what they did, no doubt, they did in a conscionable zeal, though in ignorance.

And seeing but few of the Parliament's friends understand their common freedoms, though they own the name commonwealth, therefore the Parliament's party ought to bear with the ignorance of the King's party, because they are brethren, and not make them servants, though for the present they be suffered neither to choose nor be chosen officers, lest that ignorant spirit of revenge break out in them to interrupt our common peace.

Secondly, all those who have been so hasty to buy and sell the commonwealth's land, and so to entangle it upon a new account, ought neither to choose nor be chosen officers, for hereby they declare themselves either to be for kingly interest, or else are ignorant of commonwealth's freedom, or both, therefore unfit to make laws to govern a free commonwealth, or to be overseers to see those laws executed.

What greater injury could be done to the commoners of England, than to sell away their land so hastily, before the people knew where they were, or what freedom they had got by such cost and bloodshed as they were at? And what greater ignorance could be declared by officers than to sell away the purchased land from the purchasers, or from part of them, into the hands of particular men to uphold monarchical principles?

But though this be a fault, let it be bore withal, it was ignorance of brethren; for England hath lain so long under kingly slavery that few knew what common freedom was; and let a restoration of this redeemed land be speedily made by them who have the possession of it.

For there is neither reason nor equity that a few men should go away with that land and freedom which the whole commoners have paid taxes, free-quarter and wasted their estates, healths and blood to purchase out of bondage, and many of them are in want of a comfortable livelihood.

Well, these are the men that take away other men's rights from them, and they are members of the covetous generation of self-seekers, therefore unfit to be chosen officers, or to choose.

Who then are fit to be chosen commonwealth's officers?

Why truly, choose such as have a long time given testimony by their actions to be promoters of common freedom, whether they be members in church fellowship or not in church fellowship, for all are one in Christ.

Choose such as are men of peaceable spirits, and of a peaceable conversation.

Choose such as have suffered under kingly oppression, for they will be fellow-feelers of others' bondages.

Choose such as have adventured the loss of their estates and lives to redeem the land from bondage, and who have remained constant.

Choose such as are understanding men, and who are experienced in the laws of peaceable and right-ordered government.

Choose men of courage, who are not afraid to speak the truth; for this is the shame of many in England at this day, they are drowned in the dung-hill mud of slavish fear of men; these are covetous men, not fearing God, and their portion is to be cast without the city of peace amongst the dogs.

Choose officers out of the number of those men that are above forty years of age, for these are most likely to be experienced men; and all these are likely to be men of courage, dealing truly and hating covetousness.

And if you choose men thus principled, who are poor men, as times go (for the conqueror's power hath made many a righteous man a poor man); then allow them a yearly maintenance from the common stock, until such time as a commonwealth's freedom is established, for then there will be no need of such allowances.

What is the reason that most people are so ignorant of their freedoms, and so few fit to be chosen commonwealth's officers?

Because the old kingly clergy, that are seated in parishes for lucre of tithes, are continually distilling their blind principles into the people, and do thereby nurse up ignorance in them; for they observe the bent of the people's minds, and make sermons to please the sickly minds of ignorant people, to preserve their own riches and esteem among a charmed, befooled and besotted people.

Chapter Four:

What are the Officers' Names in a free Commonwealth?

In a private family, a father or master is an officer.

In a town, city or parish,

a peace-maker.
a four-fold office of overseers.
a soldier.
a task-master.
an executioner.

In a county or shire, (This is called either the judge's court, or the county senate)

a judge.
the peace-makers of every town within that circuit.
the overseers and soldiers attending thereupon.

In a whole land:

a parliament.
a commonwealth's ministry.
a post-master.
an army.

All these offices are like links of a chain, they arise from one and the same root, which is necessity of common peace, and all their works tend to preserve common peace; therefore they are to assist each other, and all others are to assist them, as need requires, upon pain of punishment by the breach of the laws. And the rule of right government being thus observed may make a whole land, nay the whole fabric of the earth, to become one family of mankind, and one well-governed commonwealth: as Israel was called one house of Israel, though it consisted of many tribes, nations and families.

The Work of a father or master of a family:

A father is to cherish his children till they grow wise and strong, and then as a master he is to instruct them in reading, in learning languages, arts and sciences, or to bring them up to labour, or employ them in some trade or other, or cause them to be instructed therein, according as is shewed hereafter in the education of mankind.

A father is to have a care that as all his children do assist to plant the earth, or by other trades provide necessaries, so he shall see that everyone have a comfortable livelihood, not respecting one before another.

He is to command them their work and see they do it, and not suffer them to live idle; he is either to reprove by words or whip those who offend, for the rod is prepared to bring the unreasonable ones to experience and moderation:

That so children may not quarrel like beasts, but live in peace like rational men, experienced in yielding obedience to the laws and officers of the commonwealth, everyone doing to another as he would have another do to him.

The work of a peace-maker:

In a parish or town may be chosen three, four or six peacemakers, or more, according to the bigness of the place; and their work is twofold.

First, in general to sit in council to order the affairs of the parish, to prevent troubles and to preserve common peace, and here they may be called councillors.

Secondly, if there arise any matters of offence between man and man, by reason of any quarrels, disturbance or foolish actings, the offending parties shall be brought by the soldiers before any one or more of these peace-makers, who shall hear the matter and shall endeavour to reconcile the parties and make peace, and so put a stop to the rigour of the law, and go no further.

But if the peace-maker cannot persuade or reconcile the parties, then he shall command them to appear at the judge's court at the time appointed to receive the judgment of the law.

If any matters of public concernment fall out wherein the peace of the city, town or country in one county is concerned, then the peace-makers in every town thereabouts shall meet and consult about it; and from them, or from any six of them if need require, shall issue forth any order to inferior officers.

But if the matters concern only the limits of a town or city, then the peace-makers of that town shall from their court send forth orders to inferior officers for the performing of any public service within their limits.

Thirdly, if any proof be given that any officer neglects his duty, a peace-maker is to tell that officer between them two of his neglect; and if the officer continue negligent after this reproof, the peace-maker shall acquaint either the county senate or the national Parliament therewith, that from them the offender may receive condign punishment.

And it is all to this end, that the laws be obeyed; for a careful execution of laws is the life of government.

And while a peace-maker is careful to oversee the officers, all officers and others shall assist him, upon pain of forfeiture of freedom or other punishment, according to the rules following.

One thing remember, that when any offender is brought before any of these chief peace-makers, then this is to be noted, that the offender hath rejected mercy once before by refusing to yield obedience to the overseers, as is explained further hereafter.

The work of an overseer:

In a parish or town there is to be a fourfold degree of overseers, which are to be chosen yearly.

The first is an overseer to preserve peace, in case of any quarrels that may fall out between man and man; for though the earth with her fruits be a common treasury, and is to be planted and reaped by common assistance of every family, yet every house and all the furniture for ornament therein is a property to the indwellers; and when any family hath fetched in from the store-houses or shops either clothes, food or any ornament necessary for their use, it is all a property to that family.

And if any other family or man come to disturb them, and endeavour to take away furniture, which is the ornament of his neighbour's house, or to burn, break or spoil wilfully any part of his neighbours' houses, or endeavour to take away either the food or clothing which his neighbour hath provided for his use, by reason whereof quarrels and provoking words may arise:

This office of overseers is to prevent disturbance, and is an assistance to the peace-maker; and at the hearing of any such offence, this overseer shall go and hear the matter, and endeavour to persuade the offender, and to keep peace; and if friendship be made, and subjection be yielded to the laws for the peace of the commonwealth, the offender is only to be reproved for his rashness by his overseer; and there is an end.

But if the offender be so violent that he will not refrain his offence to his neighbour at this overseer's persuasion, but remain stiff and stubborn, this overseer shall then give out an order to the soldier to carry the body of the offender before the council of the peace-makers, or before any one or more of them.

And if the offender will not yield obedience to the laws of peace by the persuasion of the chief peace-makers neither, then this is to be noted to be the second time that this offender hath refused mercy.

Then shall the peace-maker appoint him a day, and command him to appear before the judge's court, either in the city or country where the offence is given, and there he shall receive sentence according to the rigour of the law.

And if an overseer should make peace, and do not send the offender to the peace-maker's court, yet this shall be noted the first time of such a one's disobedience to the laws.

And all this is to prevent quarrels and offences; and the chief peace-makers or councillors may not always be at hand at the beginning of such disturbance, therefore this overseer is an assistance thereunto, and is a member of that court.

One man shall not take away that commodity which another man hath first laid hands on, for any-commodity for use belongs to him that first laid hands on it for his use; and if another come and say, 'I will have it', and so offences do arise, this overseer shall go to them, or give order to the soldier to bring the offender to him, and shall endeavour to make peace, either by giving the commodity to him who first laid hands on it, or else by taking the commodity from both, and bid them go to the store-houses and fetch more, seeing the store-houses are full and afford plenty of the same commodities, giving the offender a sharp reproof for offering to break the peace, noting this to be the first time that such a one offered violence to break the laws of peace.

And all persons whatsoever shall assist the overseers herein; and if any person strike or affront by words this overseer, he shall give order to the soldier to carry him before the peace-makers, and from them the offender shall receive a command to appear before the judge's court, where he shall receive the sentence of the law without mitigation.

For when a peace-maker or councillor doth appoint an offender to appear before the judge's court, such an offender hath refused mercy twice.

All this is to be done in case of small offences; but if any offence be offered by any which comes within compass of death, there shall be no peace-maker to be a mediator aforehand, but the offender shall be tried by the law.

The second office of overseership is for trades:

And this overseer is to see that young people be put to masters, to be instructed in some labour, trade, science, or to be waiters in store-houses, that none shall be idly brought up in any family within his circuit.

Likewise this overseer is to assist any master of a family by his advice and counsel in the secrets of his trades, that by the experience of the elders the young people may learn the inward knowledge of the things which are, and find out the secrets of nature.

And seeing there are variety of trades, there are to be chosen overseers for every trade, so many overseers as the largeness of the town and city requires; and the employment of this overseer is not to work (unless he will himself) but to go from house to house to view the works of the people of every house belonging to his trade and circuit, and to give directions as he sees cause, and see that no youth be trained up in idleness, as is said.

And if this overseer find any youth more capable and fit for another trade than his own, he shall speak to some overseers of another trade, who shall provide him a master, with the consent of his father, and appoint him what family to live in.

And if the father of a family be weak, sick or naturally foolish, wanting the power of wisdom and government, or should be dead before his children should be instructed; then the overseers of this trade wherein the father was brought up are to put those children into such families where they may be instructed according to the law of the commonwealth.

One man may be an overseer for twenty or thirty families of shoemakers; another for smiths, another for weavers of cloth, another for the keepers of store-houses or shops; for every trade is to have an overseer for that particular trade.

And truly the government of the halls and companies in London is a very rational and well-ordered government; and the overseers of trades may very well be called masters, wardens, and assistants of such and such a company, for such and such a particular trade. Only two things are to be practised to preserve peace:

The first is, that all these overseers shall be chosen new ones every year. And secondly, the old overseers shall not choose the new ones, to prevent the creeping in of lordly oppression; but all the masters of families and freemen of that trade shall be the choosers, and the old overseers shall give but their single voice among them.

And as there are to be overseers for trades in towns and cities:

So there are to be chosen overseers in the country parishes, to see the earth planted; and in every parish in the country may be chosen four or six overseers of husbandry, to see the ground planted within their circuits, and to see that the work of husbandry be done orderly and according to reason and skill.

Some overseers to look after the shepherds, and appoint out such men as are skilled in that work. Some overseers to look after the herdsmen. Some overseers of them who look to horses, and some for the dairies. And the work of these overseers is to see that every family send in their assistance to work, both in ploughing and dressing the earth in that season of the year, in seed time; and in reaping the fruits of the earth, and housing them in store-houses in time of harvest.

Likewise they are to see that all barns belonging to any family, or more public store-houses belonging to a parish, be kept in sufficient repair. Likewise they are to see that every family do keep sufficient working tools for common use, as ploughs, carts and furniture, according as every family is furnished with men to work therewith: likewise pickaxes, spades, pruning-hooks, and any such like necessary instrument.

Likewise it is the work of this overseership to see that schoolmasters, postmasters and ministers do their several offices according to the laws.

Likewise this overseership for trades shall see that no man shall be a house-keeper, and have servants under him, till he hath served under a master seven years and hath learned his trade; and the reason is that every family may be governed by staid and experienced masters, and not by wanton youth.

And this office of overseership keeps all people within a peaceable harmony of trades, sciences or works, that there be neither beggar nor idle person in the commonwealth.

The third office of overseership is to see particular tradesmen bring in their works to store-houses and shops, and to see the waiters in store-houses do their duty.

As there are particular trades requiring strength, and some men are strong to perform such works; so there are some weak in body, whose employment shall be to be keepers of store-houses and shops, both to receive in commodities, and deliver out again, as any particular family or man wants and comes for them.

As for example:

When leather is tanned, it shall be brought into the storehouses for leather; and from thence shoemakers and harnessmakers and such like may fetch it as they need.

So for linen and woollen cloth, it is to be brought by the' weavers into the store-houses or shops, from whence particular families of other trades may fetch as they need: and so for any commodity, as in the law for store-houses is declared.

Now the work of this overseership is of the same nature with the other trades; only this is to be employed only about the oversight of store-houses and shops.

And they are to see that particular tradesmen, as weavers of linen and woollen cloth, spinners, smiths, hatters, glovers and such like, do bring in their works into the shops appointed; and they are to see that the shops and storehouses within their several circuits be kept still furnished:

That when families of other trades want such commodities as they cannot make, they may go to the shops and storehouses where such commodities are, and receive them for their use without buying or selling.

And as this officer sees the particular tradesmen to furnish the shops and store-houses, so they shall see that the keepers of the shops and store-houses be diligent to wait, both to receive in and deliver out again, according to the law, any commodity under their charge.

And if-any keeper of a shop and store-house neglect his duty of his place, through idleness or vain conversation or pride, whereby just offence is given, the overseers shall admonish him and reprove him. If he amend, all is well; if he doth not, he shall give order to the soldiers to carry him before the peace-makers' court; and if he reform upon the reproof of that court, all is well: but if he doth not reform, he shall be sent unto by the officers to appear before the judge's court, and the judge shall pass sentence, that he shall be put out of that house and employment, and sent among the husbandmen to work in the earth; and some other shall have his place and house till he be reformed.

Likewise this overseer shall see to it that the keepers of shops and store-houses do keep their houses in sufficient repair; and when any house wants repair, the keepers thereof shall speak to any of the overseers for trades, and they shall appoint either brick-layers, masons, smiths or carpenters forthwith to take the work in hand and finish it.

Fourthly, all ancient men, above sixty years of age, are general overseers

And wheresoever they go and see things amiss in any officer or tradesman, they shall call any officer or others to account for their neglect of duty to the commonwealth's peace: and these are called elders.

And everyone shall give humble respect to these as to fathers, and as to men of the highest experience in the laws for the keeping of peace in the commonwealth.

And if these see things amiss and do speak, all officers and others shall assist and protect them, to see the laws carefully executed; and everyone that affronts or abuses these in words or deeds shall suffer punishment according to the sentence of the judge.

And all these shall be general assistances and encouragers of all officers in the doing the work of their places.

And the reason of all is this that many eyes being watchful the laws may be obeyed, for to preserve peace.

But if any of these elders should vent their passion, or express envy against anyone and set up his own will above the law, and do things contrary to law, upon complaint the senators at the judge's court shall examine the matter. If he be faulty the judge shall reprove him the first time, but the second time he does so the judge shall pronounce that he shall lose his authority and never bear office nor general oversight more while he lives, only he shall have respect as a man of age.

What is the office of a soldier?

A soldier is a magistrate as well as any other officer, and indeed all state officers are soldiers, for they represent power; and if there were not power in the hand of officers, the spirit of rudeness would not be obedient to any law or government but their own wills.

Therefore every year shall be chosen a soldier, like unto a marshal of a city, and being the chief he shall have divers soldiers under him at his command, to assist in case of need.

The work of a soldier in times of peace is to fetch in offenders, and to bring them before either officer or courts, and to be a protection to the officers against all disturbances.

The soldier is not to do anything without order from the officers; but when he hath an order, then he is to act accordingly; and he is to receive orders from the judge's court or from the peace-makers' court or from overseers, as need shall require.

If a soldier hath brought an offender before a peacemaker, and if the offender will not be subject to the law by his persuasion, and the peacemaker send him to the judge's court, if the offence be under matters of death, the offender shall not be imprisoned in the mean time: but the peacemaker shall command him to appear before the judge's court at the time appointed, and the offender shall promise to obey; and this shall be for two reasons:

First, to prevent cruelty of prisons. Secondly, in the time of his binding over he may remember himself and amend his ways, and by testimony of his own actions and neighbours' reports, his sentence may be mitigated by the judge; for it is amendment not destruction that commonwealth's law requires.

And if this offender run away from that country to another, and so both disobey the peace-makers' command and break his own promise of appearance: then shall the soldiers be sent forth into all places to search for him, and if they catch him, they should bring him before the judge, who shall pronounce sentence of death upon him without mercy.

And if any protect him or shelter him, after hue and cry is made after him, all such protectors shall suffer the loss of freedom for twelve months' time, as is shewed hereafter what that is.

But if the offence should be matter of death, then the peace-maker shall take no promise from him for his appearance, but let the soldier carry him to prison till the next judge's court sits where he shall have his trial.

The work of a task-master:

The work or office of a task-master is to take those into his over-sight as are sentenced by the judge to lose their freedom, and to appoint them their work and to see they do it.

If they do their tasks, he is to allow them sufficient victuals and clothing to preserve the health of their bodies.

But if they prove desperate, wanton or idle, and will not quietly submit to the law, the task-master is to feed them with short diet, and to whip them, for a rod is prepared for the fool's back, till such time as their proud hearts do bend to the law.

And when he finds them subject, he shall then carry a favourable hand towards them, as to offending brethren, and allow them sufficient diet and clothes in hopes of their amendment, but withal see they do their work till by the sentence of the law he be set free again.

The task-master shall appoint them any kind of work or labour as he pleases that is to be done by man.

And if any of these offenders run away, there shall be hue and cry sent after him, and he shall die by the sentence of the judge when taken again.

The work of an executioner:

If any have so highly broke the laws as they come within the compass of whipping, imprisoning and death, the executioner shall cut off the head, hang or shoot to death, or whip the offender according to the sentence of law. Thus you may see what the work of every officer in a town or city is.

What is the work of a judge?

The law itself is the judge of all men's actions, yet he who is chosen to pronounce the law is called judge, because he is the mouth of the law: for no single man ought to judge or interpret the law:

Because the law itself, as it is left us in the letter, is the mind and determination of the Parliament and of the people of the land, to be their rule to walk by and to be the touchstone of all actions.

And that man who takes upon him to interpret the law doth either darken the sense of the law, and so makes it confused and hard to be understood, or else puts another meaning upon it, and so lifts up himself above the Parliament, above the law, and above all people in the land.

Therefore the work of that man who is called judge is to hear any matter that is brought before him; and in all cases of difference between man and man, he shall see the parties on both sides before him, and shall hear each man speak for himself without a fee'd lawyer; likewise he is to examine any witness who is to prove a matter in trial before him.

And then he is to pronounce the bare letter of the law concerning such a thing, for he hath his name 'judge' not because his will and mind is to judge the actions of offenders before him, but because he is the mouth to pronounce the law, who indeed is the true judge. Therefore to this law and to this testimony let everyone have a regard who intends to live in peace in the commonwealth.

But from hence hath arose much misery in the nations under kingly government, in that the man called the judge hath been suffered to interpret the law; and when the mind of the law, the judgment of the Parliament and the government of the land, is resolved into the breast of the judges this bath occasioned much complaining of injustice in judges, in courts of justice, in lawyers, and in the course of the law itself, as if it were an evil rule.

Because the law, which was a certain rule, was varied according to the will of a covetous, envious or proud judge, therefore no marvel though the kingly laws be so intricate, and though few know which way the course of the law goes, because the sentence lies many times in the breast of a judge, and not in the letter of the law.

And so the good laws made by an industrious Parliament are like good eggs laid by a silly gooses and as soon as she hath laid them, she goes her way and lets others take them, and never looks after them more, so that if you lay a stone in her nest, she will sit upon it as if it were an egg.

And so though the laws be good, yet if they be left to the will of a judge to interpret, the execution hath many times proved bad.

And truly as the laws and people of nations have been abused by suffering men (judges) to alter the sense by their interpretation:

So likewise hath the Scriptures of Moses, the prophets, Christ and his apostles been darkened and confounded by suffering ministers to put their inferences and interpretations upon them.

And surely both the judges for the law and the ministers for God's Word have been both unfaithful servants to man and to God, by taking upon them to expound and interpret that rule which they are bound to yield obedience to, without adding to or diminishing from.

What is the judge's court?

In a county or shire there is to be chosen

a judge,
the peace-makers of every town within that circuit,
the overseers, and
a band of soldiers attending thereupon.

And this is called the judge's court or the county senate. This court shall sit four times in the year (or oftener if need be) in the country, and four times in the year in great cities. In the first quarter of the year they shall sit in the east part of the county, and the second quarter of the year in the west, in the third in the south and in the fourth in the north.

And this court is to oversee and examine any officer within their county or limits; for their work is to see that everyone be faithful in his place; and if any officer hath done wrong to any, this court is to pass sentence of punishment upon the offender, according to his offence against the law.

If any grievance lie upon any man, wherein inferior officers cannot ease him, this court shall quietly hear his complaint, and ease him; for where a law is wanting, they may prepare a way of ease for the offender till the Parliament sit, who may either establish that conclusion for a law, if they approve of it, or frame another law to that effect; for it is possible that many things may fall out hereafter which the law-makers for the present may not foresee.

If any disorder break in among the people, this court shall set things to rights. If any be bound over to appear at this court, the judge shall hear the matter and pronounce the letter of the law, according to the nature of the offence.

So that the alone work of the judge is-to pronounce the sentence and mind of the law; and all this is but to see the laws executed, that the peace of the commonwealth may be preserved.

What is the work of a commonwealth's Parliament in general?

A Parliament is the highest court of equity in a land, and it is to be chosen every year; and out of every city, town and certain limits of a country through the land, two, three or more men are to be chosen to make up this court.

This court is to oversee all other courts, officers, persons and actions, and to have a full power, being the representative of the whole land, to remove all grievances and to ease the people that are oppressed.

A Parliament hath his rise from the lowest office in a commonwealth, viz. from the father in a family. For as a father's tender care is to remove all grievances from the oppressed children, not respecting one before another; so a Parliament are to remove all burdens from the people of the land, and are not to respect persons who are great before them who are weak; but their eye and care must be principally to relieve the oppressed ones, who groan under the tyrants' laws and power. The strong, or such as have the tyrant power to uphold them, need no help.

But though a Parliament be the father of a land, yet by the covetousness and cheats of kingly government the heart of this father hath been alienated from the children of the Land, or else so over-awed by the frowns of a kingly tyrant :hat they could not or durst not act for the weakest children's ease.

For hath not Parliaments sat and rose again and made Laws to strengthen the tyrant in his throne, and to strengthen the rich and the strong by those laws, and left Oppression upon the backs of the oppressed still?

But I'll not reap up former weaknesses, but rather rejoice in hope of amendment, seeing our present Parliament hath declared England to be a free commonwealth, and to cast out kingly power; and upon this ground I rejoice in hope that succeeding Parliaments will be tender-hearted fathers to the oppressed children of the land;

And not only dandle us upon the knee with good words and promises till particular men's turns be served, but will Fill our bellies and clothe our backs with good actions of Freedom, and give to the oppressed children's children their birthright portion, which is freedom in the commonwealth's land, which the kingly law and power, our cruel step-fathers and step-mothers, have kept from us and our fathers for many years past.

The particular work of a Parliament is fourfold:

First, as a tender father, a Parliament is to empower officers and give out orders for the free planting and reaping of the commonwealth's land, that all who have been oppressed and kept from the free use thereof by conquerors, kings and their tyrant laws may now be set at liberty to plant in freedom for food and raiment; and are to be a protection to them who labour the earth, and a punisher of them who are idle. But some may say, 'What is that I call commonwealth's land?'

I answer, all that land which hath been withheld from the inhabitants by the conqueror or tyrant kings, and is now recovered out of the hands of that oppression by the joint assistance of the persons and purses of the commoners of the land; for this land is the price of their blood. It is their birthright to them and their posterity, and ought not to be converted into particular hands again by the laws of a free commonwealth.

And in particular, this land is all abbey lands, formerly recovered out of the hands of the pope's power by the blood of the commoners of England, though the kings withheld their rights herein from them.

So likewise all crown lands, bishops' lands, with all parks, forests, chases, now of late recovered out of the hands of the kingly tyrants, who have set lords of manors and taskmasters over the commoners to withhold the free use of the land from them.

So likewise all the commons and waste lands, which are called commons because the poor was to have part therein; but this is withheld from the commoners, either by lords of manors requiring quit rents and overseeing the poor so narrowly that none dares build him a house upon this common land, or plant thereupon without his leave, but must pay him rent, fines and heriots and homage, as unto a conqueror; or else the benefit of this common land is taken away from the younger brethren by rich landlords and freeholders, who overstock the commons with sheep and cattle, so that the poor in many places are not able to keep a cow unless they steal grass for her.

And this is the bondage the poor complain of, that they are kept poor by their brethren in a land where there is so much plenty for everyone, if covetousness and pride did not rule as king in one brother over another, and kingly government occasions all this.

Now it is the work of a Parliament to break the tyrants' bonds, to abolish all their oppressing laws, and to give orders, encouragements and directions unto the poor oppressed people of the land, that they forthwith plant and manure this their own land for the free and comfortable livelihood of themselves and posterities;

And to declare to them, it is their own creation rights, faithfully and courageously recovered by their diligence, purses and blood from under the kingly tyrants' and oppressors' power.

The work of a Parliament, secondly,

Is to abolish all old laws and customs which have been the strength of the oppressor, and to prepare and then to enact new laws for the ease and freedom of the people, but yet not without the people's knowledge.

For the work of a Parliament herein is threefold.

First, when old laws and customs of the kings do burden the people, and the people desire the remove of them and the establishment of more easy laws:

It is now the work of a Parliament to search into reason and equity, how relief may be found out for the people in such a case, and to preserve a common peace; and when they have found out a way by debate of counsel among themselves, whereby the people may be relieved, they are not presently to establish their conclusions for a law.

But in the next place, they are to make a public declaration thereof to the people of the land who choose them, for their approbation; and if no objection come in from the people within one month, they may then take the people's silence as a consent thereto.

And then in the third place they are to enact it for a law, to be a binding rule to the whole land. For as the remove of the old laws and customs are by the people's consent, which is proved by their frequent petitioning and requests of such a thing: so the enacting of new laws must be by the people's consent and knowledge likewise.

And here they are to require the consent, not of men interested in the old oppressing laws and customs, as kings used to do, but of them who have been oppressed. And the reason is this:

Because the people must be all subject to the law, under pain of punishment; therefore it is all reason they should know it before it be enacted, that if there be any thing of the counsel of oppression in it, it may be discovered and amended.

But you will say, 'If it must be so, then will men so differ in their judgments, that we shall never agree'. I answer:

There is but bondage and freedom, particular interest or common interest; and he who pleads to bring in particular interest into a free commonwealth will presently be seen and cast out, as one bringing in kingly slavery again.

And men in place and office, where greatness and honour is coming in, may sooner be corrupted to bring in particular interest than a whole land can be, who must either suffer sorrow under a burdensome law, or rejoice under a law of freedom.

And surely those men who are not willing to enslave the people will not be unwilling to consent hereunto.

The work of a Parliament, thirdly,

Is to see all those burdens removed actually, which have hindered or do hinder the oppressed people from the enjoyment of their birthrights.

If their common lands be under the oppression of lords of manors, they are to see the land freed from that slavery.

If the commonwealth's land be sold by the hasty counsel of subtle, covetous and ignorant officers, who act for their own particular interest, and so hath entangled the commoners' land again under colour of being bought and sold:

A Parliament is to examine what authority any had to sell or buy the commonwealth land without a general consent of the people; for it is not any one's but everyone's birthright. And if some through covetousness and self-interest gave consent privately, yet a Parliament, who is the father of a land, ought not to give consent to buy and sell that land which is all the children's birthright and the price of their labours, monies and blood.

They are to declare likewise that the bargain is unrighteous, and that the buyers and sellers are enemies to the peace and freedom of the commonwealth. For indeed the necessity of the people chose a Parliament to help them in their weakness; and where they see a danger like to impoverish or enslave one part of the people to another, they are to give warning and so prevent that danger; for they are the eyes of the land. And surely those are blind eyes that lead the people into bogs, to be entangled in mud again after they are once pulled out.

And when the land is once freed from the oppressors' power and laws, a Parliament is to keep it so, and not suffer it by their consent to have it bought or sold, and so entangled in bondage upon a new account.

And for their faithfulness herein to the people, the people are engaged by love and faithfulness to cleave close to them, in defence and protection. But when a Parliament have no care herein, the hearts of the people run away from them like sheep who have no shepherd.

All grievances are occasioned either by the covetous wills of state-officers, who neglect their obedience to the good laws, and then prefer their own ease, honour and riches before the ease and freedom of the oppressed people. And here a Parliament is to cashier and punish those officers, and place others who are men of public spirits in their rooms:

Or else the people's grievances arise from the practice and power that the kings' laws have given to lords of manors, covetous landlords, tithe-takers or unbounded lawyers, being all strengthened in their oppressions over the people by that kingly law. And when the people are burdened herewith and groan, waiting for deliverance, as the oppressed people of England do at this day; it is then the work of a Parliament to see the people delivered, and that they enjoy their creation freedoms in the earth. They are not to dally with them, but as a father is ready to help his children out of misery, when they either see them in misery or when the children cry for help; so should they do for the oppressed people.

And surely for this end, and no other, is a Parliament chosen, as is cleared before: for the necessity of common preservation and peace is the fundamental law both to officers and people.

The work of a Parliament, fourthly, is this:

If there be an occasion to raise an army to wage war, either against an invasion of a foreign enemy or against an insurrection at home, it is the work of a Parliament to manage that business for to preserve common peace. And here their work is threefold:

First, to acquaint the people plainly with the cause of the war, and to shew them the danger of such an invasion or insurrection; and so from that cause require their assistance in person for the preservation of the laws, liberties and peace of the commonwealth, according to their engagement when they were chosen, which was this: do you maintain our laws and liberties, and we will protect and assist you.

Secondly, a Parliament is to make choice of understanding, able and public-spirited men to be leaders of an army in this case, and to give them commissions and power in the name of the commonwealth to manage the work of an army.

Thirdly, a Parliament's work in this case is either to send ambassadors to another nation which hath invaded our land, or that intends to invade, to agree upon terms of peace, or to proclaim war; or else to receive and hear ambassadors from other lands for the same business, or about any other business concerning the peace and honour of the land.

For a Parliament is the head of a commonwealth's power, or (as it may be said) it is the great council of an army, from whom originally all orders do issue forth to any officer or soldier.

For if so be a Parliament had not an army to protect them, the rudeness of the people would not obey their proceedings: and if a Parliament were not the representative of the people, who indeed is the body of ail power, the army would not obey their orders.

So then, a Parliament is the head of power in a commonwealth, and it is their work to manage public affairs, in times of war and in times of peace; not to promote the interest of particular men, but for the peace and freedom of the whole body of the land, viz. of every particular man, that none be deprived of his creation rights unless he hath lost his freedom by transgression, as by the laws is expressed.

The work of a commonwealth's ministry, and why one day in seven may be a day of rest from labour:

If there were good laws, and the people be ignorant of them, it would be as bad for the commonwealth as if there were no laws at all.

Therefore according to one of the laws of Israel's commonwealth made by Moses, who was the ruler of the people at that time:

It is very rational and good that one day in seven be still set apart, for three reasons:

First, that the people in such a parish may generally meet together to see one another's faces, and beget or preserve fellowship in friendly love;

Secondly, to be a day of rest or cessation from labour, so that they have some bodily rest for themselves and cattle;

Thirdly, that he who is chosen minister (for that year) in that parish may read to the people three things:

First the affairs of the whole land, as it is brought in by the postmaster (as it is related in his office, hereafter following).

Secondly, to read the law of the commonwealth: not only to strengthen the memory of the ancients, but that the young people also, who are not grown up to ripeness of experience, may be instructed to know when they do well and when they do ill; for the laws of a land hath the power of freedom and bondage, life and death, in its hand, therefore the necessary knowledge to be known, and he is the best prophet that acquaints men therewith: that as men grow up in years, they may be able to defend the laws and government of the land. But these laws shall not be expounded by the reader, for to expound a plain law, as if a man would put a better meaning than the letter itself, produces two evils:

First the pure law and the minds of people will be thereby confounded, for multitude of words darken knowledge;

Secondly the reader will be puffed up in pride, to contemn the lawmakers, and in time that will prove the father and nurse of tyranny, as at this day is manifested by our ministry;

And thirdly because the minds of people generally love discourses, therefore that the wits of men both young and old may be exercised, there may be speeches made in a threefold nature.

First to declare the acts and passages of former ages and governments, setting forth the benefit of freedom by well-ordered governments, as in Israel's commonwealth, and the troubles and bondage which hath always attended oppression and oppressors; as the state of Pharaoh and other tyrant kings, who said the earth and people were theirs and only at their dispose.

Secondly speeches may be made of all arts and sciences, some one day, some another: as in physic, chirurgery, astrology, astronomy, navigation, husbandry and such like. And in these speeches may be unfolded the nature of all herbs and plants from the hyssop to the cedar, as Solomon writ of.

Likewise men may come to see into the nature of the fixed and wandering stars, those great powers of God in the heavens above; and hereby men will come to know the secrets of nature and creation, within which all true knowledge is wrapped up, and the light in man must arise to search it out.

Thirdly speeches may be made sometimes of the nature of mankind, of his darkness and of his light, of his weakness and of his strength, of his love and of his envy, of his sorrow and of his joy, of his inward and outward bondages, and of his inward and outward freedoms, etc. And this is that which the ministry of churches generally aim at, but, only that they confound their knowledge by imaginary study, when anyone takes upon him to speak without experience.

Now this is the way to attain to the true knowledge of God (who is the spirit of the whole creation) as he hath spread himself forth in every form, and more eminently in man; as Paul writ, The creation in all the several bodies and forms are but the mansions or fulness of him who hath filled all things with himself.

And if the earth were set free from kingly bondage, so that everyone were sure to have a free livelihood, and if this liberty were granted, then many secrets of God, and his works in nature, would be made public, which men nowadays keep secret to get a living by: so that this kingly bondage is the cause of the spreading of ignorance in the earth. But when commonwealth's freedom is established, and Pharisaical or kingly slavery cast out, then will knowledge cover the earth, as the waters cover the seas; and not till then.

He who is the chosen minister for that year to read shall not be the only man to make sermons or speeches; but everyone who hath any experience, and is able to speak of any art or language or of the nature of the heavens above or of the earth below, shall have free liberty to speak when they offer themselves, and in a civil manner desire an audience, and appoint his day. yet he who is the reader may have his liberty to speak too, but not to assume all the power to himself, as the proud and ignorant clergy have done, who have bewitched all the world by their subtle covetousness and pride.

And everyone who speaks of any herb, plant, art or nature of mankind, is required to speak nothing by imagination, but what he hath found out by his own industry and observation in trial.

And because other nations are of several languages, therefore these speeches may be made sometimes in other languages, and sometimes in our mother tongue, that so the men of our English commonwealth may attain to all knowledges, arts and languages, and that everyone may be encouraged in his industry, and purchase the countenance and love of their neighbourhood for their wisdom and experimental knowledge in the things which are.

And thus to speak, or thus to read the law of nature (or God) as he hath written his name in every body, is to speak a pure language, and this is to speak the truth as Jesus Christ spake it, giving to everything its own weight and measure.

By this means in time men shall attain to the practical knowledge of God truly, that they may serve him in spirit and truth; and this knowledge will not deceive a man.

'Aye but,' saith the zealous but ignorant professor,

'This is a low and carnal ministry indeed, this leads men to know nothing but the knowledge of the earth and the secrets of nature, but we are to look after spiritual and heavenly things.' I answer:

To know the secrets of nature is to know the works of God; and to know the works of God within the creation is to know God himself, for God dwells in every visible work or body.

And indeed if you would know spiritual things, it is to know how the spirit or power of wisdom and life, causing motion or growth, dwells within and governs both the several bodies of the stars and planets in the heavens above, and the several bodies of the earth below, as grass, plants, fishes, beasts, birds and mankind; for to reach God beyond the creation, or to know what he will be to a man after the man is dead, if any otherwise than to scatter him into his essences of fire, water, earth and air of which he is compounded, is a knowledge beyond the line or capacity of man to attain to while he lives in his compounded body.

And if a man should go to imagine what God is beyond the creation, or what he will be in a spiritual demonstration after a man is dead, he doth (as the proverb saith) build castles in the air, or tells us of a world beyond the moon and beyond the sun, merely to blind the reason of man.

I'll appeal to yourself in this question, what other knowledge have you of God but what you have within the circle of the creation?

For if the creation in all its dimensions be the fulness of him that fills all with himself, and if you yourself be part of this creation, where can you find God but in that line or station wherein you stand?

God manifests himself in actual knowledge, not in imagination; he is still in motion, either in bodies upon earth, or in the bodies in the heavens, or in both; in the night and in the day, in winter, in summer, in cold, in heat, in growth or not in growth.

But when a studying imagination comes into man, which is the devil, for it is the cause of all evil and sorrows in the world: that is he who puts out the eyes of man's knowledge, and tells him he must believe what others have writ or spoke, and must not trust to his own experience. And when this bewitching fancy sits in the chair of government, there is nothing but saying and unsaying, frowardness, covetousness, fears, confused thoughts and unsatisfied doubtings, all the days of that man's reign in the heart.

Or secondly, examine yourself, and look likewise into the ways of all professors, and you shall find that the enjoyment of the earth below, which you call a low and a carnal knowledge, is that which you and all professors (as well as the men of the world, as you call them) strive and seek after.

Wherefore are you so covetous after the world, in buying and selling? counting yourself a happy man if you be rich, and a miserable man if you be poor. And though you say, heaven after death is a place of glory, where you shall enjoy God face to face, yet you are loath to leave the earth to go thither.

Do not your ministers preach for to enjoy the earth? Do not professing lawyers, as well as others, buy and sell the conqueror's justice, that they may enjoy the earth? Do not professing soldiers fight for the earth, and seat themselves in that land which is the birthright of others as well as theirs, shutting others out? Do not all professors strive to get earth, that they may live in plenty by other men's labours?

Do you not make the earth your very rest? Doth not the enjoying of the earth please the spirit in you? And then you say, God is pleased with your ways and blesseth you. If you want earth and become poor, do you not say, God is angry with you and crosseth you?

Why do you heap up riches? Why do you eat and drink and wear clothes? Why do you take a woman and lie with her to beget children? Are not all these carnal and low things of the earth? And do you not live in them, and covet them as much as any? nay more than many which you call men of the world?

And it being thus with you, what other spiritual or heavenly things do you seek after more than others? And what is in you more than in others? If you say, 'There is'; then surely you ought to let these earthly things alone to the men of the world, as you call them, whose portions these are; and keep you within the compass of your own sphere, that others seeing you live a life above the world in peace and freedom, neither working yourself nor deceiving, nor compelling others to work for you, they may be drawn to embrace the same spiritual life by your single-hearted conversation. Well, I have done here.

Let us now examine your divinity:

Which you call heavenly and spiritual things, for herein speeches are made not to advance knowledge, but to destroy the true knowledge of God. For divinity does not speak the truth as it is hid in every body, but it leaves the motional knowledge of a thing as it is and imagines, studies or thinks what may be, and so runs the hazard, true or false. And this divinity is always speaking words to deceive the simple, that he may make them work for him and maintain him, but he never comes to action himself to do as he would be done by; for he is a monster who is all tongue and no hand.

This divining doctrine, which you call spiritual and heavenly things, is the thief and the robber. He comes to spoil the vineyard of a man's peace, and does not enter in at the door but he climbs up another way. And this doctrine is twofold.

First he takes upon him to tell you the meaning of other men's words and writing by his studying or imagining what another man's knowledge might be, and by thus doing darkens knowledge and wrongs the spirit of the authors who did write and speak those things which he takes upon him to interpret.

Secondly he takes upon him to foretell what shall befall a man after he is dead, and what that world is beyond the sun and beyond the moon, etc. And if any man tell him there is no reason for what you say, he answers, 'You must not judge of heavenly and spiritual things by reason, but you must believe what is told you, whether it be reason or no'. There is a threefold discovery of falsehood in this doctrine.

For first it is a doctrine of a sickly and weak spirit, who hath lost his understanding in the knowledge of the creation and of the temper of his own heart and nature, and so runs into fancies, either of joy or sorrow.

And if the passion of joy predominate, then he fancies to himself a personal God, personal angels and a local place of glory which, he saith, he and all who believes what he saith shall go to after they are dead.

And if sorrow predominate, then he fancies to himself a personal devil and a local place of torment, that he shall go to after he is dead, and this he speaks with great confidence.

Or secondly, this is the doctrine of a subtle running spirit, to make an ungrounded wise man mad: that he might be called the more excellent man in knowledge. For many times when a wise understanding heart is assaulted with this doctrine of a God, a devil, a heaven and a hell, salvation and damnation after a man is dead, his spirit being not strongly grounded in the knowledge of the creation, nor in the temper of his own heart, he strives and stretches his brains to find out the depth of that doctrine and cannot attain to it: for indeed it is not knowledge but imagination; and so, by poring and puzzling himself in it, loses that wisdom he had, and becomes distracted and mad. And if the passion of joy predominate, then he is merry and sings and laughs, and is ripe in the expressions of his words and will speak strange things: but all by imagination. But if the passion of sorrow predominate, then he is heavy and sad, crying out, He is damned, God hath forsaken him and he must go to hell when he dies, he cannot make his calling and election sure. And in that distemper many times a man doth hang, kill or drown himself; so that this divining doctrine, which you call 'spiritual and heavenly things' torments people always when they are weak, sickly and under any distemper; therefore it cannot be the doctrine of Christ the saviour.

For my own part, my spirit hath waded deep to find the bottom of this divining spiritual doctrine: and the more I searched, the more I was at a loss; and I never came to quiet rest, and to know God in my spirit, till I came to the knowledge of the things in this book. And let me tell you, they who preach this divining doctrine are the murderers of many a poor heart who is bashful and simple, and that cannot speak for himself-but that keeps his thoughts to himself.

Or thirdly, this doctrine is made a cloak of policy by the subtle elder brother, to cheat his simple younger brother of the freedoms of the earth. For, saith the elder brother, 'The earth is mine and not yours, brother; and you must not work upon it unless you will hire it of me;

and you must not take the fruits of it unless you will buy them of me, by that which I pay you for your labour. For if you should do otherwise, God will not love you, and you shall not go to heaven when you die, but the devil will have you and you must be damned in hell.'

If the younger reply and say, 'The earth is my birthright as well as yours, and God who made us both is no respecter of persons: therefore there is no reason but I should enjoy the freedoms of the earth for my comfortable livelihood as well as you; brother.'

'Aye but', saith the elder brother, 'you must not trust to your own reason and understanding, but you must believe what is written and what is told you; and if you will not believe, your damnation will be the greater.'

'I cannot believe', saith the younger brother, 'that our righteous creator should be so partial in his dispensations of the earth, seeing our bodies cannot live upon earth without the use of the earth.'

The elder brother replies, 'What, will you be an atheist and a factious man? Will you not believe God?'

'Yes,' saith the younger brother, 'if I knew God said so I should believe, for I desire to serve him.'

'Why,' saith the elder brother, 'this is his Word, and if you will not believe it, you must be damned; but if you will believe it, you must go to heaven.'

Well, the younger brother, being weak in spirit and having not a grounded knowledge of the creation nor of himself, is terrified and lets go his hold in the earth, and submits himself to be a slave to his brother for fear of damnation in hell after death, and in hopes to get heaven thereby after he is dead; and so his eyes are put out, and his reason is blinded.

So that this divining spiritual doctrine is a cheat; for while men are gazing up to heaven, imagining after a happiness or fearing a hell after they are dead, their eyes are put out? that they see not what is their birthrights, and what is to be done by them here on earth while they are living. This is the filthy dreamer, and the cloud without rain.

And indeed the subtle clergy do know that if they can but charm the people, by this their divining doctrine, to look after riches, heaven and glory when they are dead, that then they shall easily be the inheritors of the earth, and have the deceived people to be their servants.

This divining doctrine, which you call spiritual and heavenly, was not the doctrine of Christ; for his words were pure knowledge, they were words of life. For he said, He spoke what he had seen with his Father; for he had the knowledge of the creation, and spake as everything was.

And this divinity came in after Christ to darken his knowledge; and it is the language of the mystery of iniquity and Antichrist, whereby the covetous, ambitious and serpentine spirit cozens the plain-hearted of his portions in the earth.

And divinity cozens a plain heart two ways. First, if a man have an estate, according to the kings' laws, he is made by this charm to give it or bazle [2] it away to the priests or to religious uses, in hopes to get heaven when he is dead.

Or secondly, a man by running to hear divinity sermons, and dancing after his charming pipe, neglects his labour and so runs into debt, and then his fellow professors will cast him into prison and starve him there, and their divinity will call him a hypocrite and wicked man, and become a devil to torment him in that hell.

But surely light is so broke out that it will cover the earth, so that the divinity charmers shall say, The people will not hear the voice of our charming, charm we never so wisely. And all the priests and clergy and preachers of these spiritual and heavenly things, as they call them, shall take up the lamentation, which is their portion, Alas, alas, that great city Babylon, that mighty city divinity, which hath filled the whole earth with her sorcery and deceived all people, so that the whole world wondered after this Beast; how is it fallen, and how is her judgment come upon her in one hour? And further, as you may read, Rev. 18.10.

The officer of the postmaster:

In every parish throughout the commonwealth shall be chosen two men (at the time when other officers are chosen), and these shall be called postmasters. And whereas there are four parts of the land, east, west, north, south, there shall be chosen in the chief city two men to receive in what the postmaster of the east country brings in, and two men to receive in what the postmaster of the west brings in, and two for the north, and so two for the south.

Now the work of the country postmaster shall be this: they shall every month bring up or send by tidings from their respective parishes to the chief city, of what accidents or passages fall out which is either to the honour or dishonour, hurt or profit, of the commonwealth; and if nothing have fallen out in that month worth observation, then they shall write down peace or good order in such a parish.

And when these respective postmasters have brought up their bills or certificates from all parts of the land, the receivers of those bills shall write down everything in order from parish to parish in the nature of a weekly bill of observation.

And those eight receivers shall cause the affairs of the four quarters of the land to be printed in one book with what speed may be, and deliver to every postmaster a book, that as they bring up the affairs of one parish in writing, they may carry down in print the affairs of the whole land.

The benefit lies here, that if any part of the land be visited with plague, famine, invasion or insurrection, or any casualties, the other parts of the land may have speedy knowledge, and send relief.

And if any accident fall out through unreasonable action or careless neglect, other parts of the land may thereby be made watchful to prevent like danger.

Or if any through industry or ripeness of understanding have found out any secret in nature, or new invention in any art or trade or in the tillage of the earth, or such like, whereby the commonwealth may more flourish in peace and plenty, for which virtues those persons received honour in the places where they dwelt:

When other parts of the land hear of it, many thereby will be encouraged to employ their reason and industry to do the like, that so in time there will not be any secret in nature which now lies hid (by reason of the iron age of kingly oppressing government) but by some or other will be brought to light, to the beauty of our commonwealth.

The rise of a commonwealth's army:

After that the necessity of the people in a parish, in a county and in a land, hath moved the people to choose officers to preserve common peace, the same necessity causeth the people to say to their officers,

'Do you see our laws observed for our common preservation, and we will assist and protect you.'

This word 'assist' and 'protect' implies the rising of the people by force of arms to defend their laws and officers, who rule well, against any invasion, insurrection or rebellion of selfish officers or rude people; yea to beat down the turbulency of any foolish spirit that shall arise to break our common peace.

So that the same law of necessity of common peace, which moved the people to choose officers and to compose a law for to be a rule of government, the same law of necessity of protection doth raise an army; so that an army, as well as other officers in a commonwealth, spring from one and the same root, viz. from the necessity of common preservation.

An army is twofold, viz. a ruling army or a fighting army.

A ruling army is called magistracy in times of peace, keeping that land and government in peace by execution of the laws, which the fighting army did purchase in the field by their blood out of the hands of oppression.

And here all officers, from the father in a family to the parliament in a land, are but the heads and leaders of an army; and all people arising to protect and assist their officers, in defence of a right-ordered government, are but the body of an army.

And this magistracy is called the rejoicing of all nations, when the foundation thereof are laws of common equity, whereby every single man may enjoy the fruit of his labour in the free use of the earth, without being restrained or oppressed by the hands of others.

Secondly, a fighting army, called soldiers in the field, when the necessity of preservation, by reason of a foreign invasion or inbred oppression, do move the people to arise in an army to cut and tear to pieces either degenerated officers, or rude people who seek their own interest and not common freedom, and through treachery do endeavour to destroy the laws of common freedom, and to enslave both the land and people of the commonwealth to their particular wills and lusts.

And this war is called a plague, because that cursed enmity of covetousness, pride and vain-glory and envy in the heart of mankind did occasion the rise of it, because he will not be under the moderate observation of any free and right order unless he himself be king and lord over other persons and their labours.

For now the people do arise to defend their faithful officers against such officers as are unfaithful, and to defend their laws and common peace.

The use or work of a fighting army in a commonwealth…

Is to beat down all that arise to endeavour to destroy the liberties of the commonwealth. For as, in the days of monarchy, an army was used to subdue all who rebelled against kingly property, so in the days of a free commonwealth an army is to be made use of to resist and destroy all who endeavour to keep up or bring in kingly bondage again.

The work of this fighting army is twofold.

The first is to withstand the invasion or coming in of a foreign enemy, whose invasion is for no other end but to take away our land and earth from us, to deny us the free use thereof, to become kings and landlords over us and to make us their slaves.

As William the Conqueror when he had conquered England, he gave not only the land in parcels to his soldiers, but he gave all men, their wives and children within such a lordship to his lords of manors, to do with them as they pleased. And for this cause now doth an army arise to keep out an invasion of a foreigner, that by the defence of our army, who is part of ourselves, the rest of our brethren in the commonwealth may plough, sow and reap, and enjoy the fruits of their labours, and so live in peace in their own land.

Or secondly, if a land be conquered and so enslaved as England was under the kings and conquering laws, then an army is to be raised with as much secrecy as may be, to restore the land again and set it free, that the earth may become a common treasury to all her children, without respecting persons, as it was before kingly bondage came in, as you may read, I Sam. 8.

This latter is called civil wars, and this is the wars of the commoners of England against King Charles now cast out, for he and his laws were the successive power of that Norman conquest over England.

And now the commoners of England in this age of the world are rise up in an army, and have cast out that invasion of the Duke of Normandy and have won their land and liberties again by the sword, if they do not suffer their counsels to befool them into slavery again upon a new account.

Therefore you army of England's commonwealth, look to it! The enemy could not beat you in the field, but they may be too hard for you by policy in counsel, if you do not stick close to see common freedom established.

For if so be that kingly authority be set up in your laws again, King Charles hath conquered you and your posterity by policy and won the field of you, though you seemingly have cut off his head.

For the strength of a king lies not in the visible appearance of his body, but in his will, laws and authority, which is called monarchical government.

But if you remove kingly government and set up true and free commonwealth's government, then you gain your crown, and keep it, and leave peace to your posterity, otherwise not.

And thus doing makes a war either lawful or unlawful.

An army may be murderers and unlawful.

If an army be raised to cast out kingly oppression, and if the heads of that army promise a commonwealth's freedom to the oppressed people if in case they will assist with person and purse, and if the people do assist, and prevail over the tyrant, those officers are bound by the law of justice (who is God) to make good their engagements. And if they do not set the land free from the branches of the kingly oppression, but reserve some part of the kingly power to advance their own particular interest, whereby some of their friends are left under as great slavery to them as they were under the kings, those officers are not faithful commonwealth's soldiers, they are worse thieves and tyrants than the kings they cast out; and that honour they seemed to get by their victories over the commonwealth's oppressor they lose again by breaking promise and engagement to their oppressed friends who did assist them.

For what difference is there between a professed tyrant, that declares himself a tyrant in words, laws and deeds, as all conquerors do, and him who promises to free me from the power of the tyrant if I'll assist him; and when I have spent my estate and blood and the health of my body, and expect my bargain by his engagements to me, he sits himself down in the tyrant's chair and takes the possession of the land to himself, and calls it his and none of mine, and tells me he cannot in conscience let me enjoy the freedom of the earth with him, because it is another man's right?

And now my health and estate is decayed, and I grow in age, I must either beg or work for day wages, which I was never brought up to, for another; whenas the earth is as freely my inheritance and birthright as his whom I must work for; and if I cannot live by my weak labours but take where I need, as Christ sent and took the ass's colt in his need, there is no dispute but by the kings and laws he will hang me for a thief.

But hear, O thou righteous spirit of the whole creation, and judge who is the thief: him who takes away the freedom of the common earth from me, which is my creation rights and which I have helped to purchase out of the hands of the kingly oppressor by my purse and person, and which he hath taken for wages of me;

Or I, who takes the common earth to plant upon for my free livelihood, endeavouring to live as a free commoner in a free commonwealth, in righteousness and peace.

Such a soldier as this engagement-breaker is neither a friend to the creation nor to a particular commonwealth, but a self-lover and a hypocrite, for he did not fight to set the earth free from the bondage of the oppressor as he pretended by his engagements: but to remove that power out of the other's hand into his own. And this is just like the beasts who fight for mastery and keeps it, not relieving but still lording and kinging over the weak. These are monarchical soldiers not commonwealth's soldiers; and such a soldier is a murderer and his warfare is unlawful.

But soldiers of true noble spirits will help the weak and set the oppressed free, and delight to see the commonwealth flourish in freedom, as well as their own gardens. There is none of this true nobility in the monarchical army, for they are all self-lovers; the best is as a briar, and the most upright amongst them is as a thorn held. Speak you prophets of old if this be not true.

A monarchical army lifts up mountains and makes valleys, viz. advances tyrants and treads the oppressed in the barren lanes of poverty.

But a commonwealth's army is like John Baptist, who levels the mountains to the valleys, pulls down the tyrant and lifts up the oppressed: and so makes way for the spirit of peace and freedom to come in to rule and inherit the earth.

And by this which hath been spoken, an army may see wherein they may do well, and wherein they may do hurt.

Chapter Five:

Education of mankind, in Schools and Trades

Mankind in the days of his youth is like a young colt, wanton and foolish, till he be broke by education and correction; and the neglect of this care, or the want of wisdom in the performance of it, hath been and is the cause of much division and trouble in the world.

Therefore the law of a commonwealth does require that not only a father but that all overseers and officers should make it their work to educate children in good manners, and to see them brought up in some trade or other, and to suffer no children in any parish to live in idleness and youthful pleasure all their days, as many have been, but that they be brought up like men and not like beasts: that so the commonwealth may be planted with laborious and wise experienced men, and not with idle fools.

Mankind may be considered in a fourfold degree, his childhood, youth, manhood and old age. His childhood and his youth may be considered from his birth till forty years of age; and within this compass of time, after he is weaned from his mother, who shall be the nurse herself if there be no defect in nature, his parents shall teach him a civil and humble behaviour toward all men. Then send him to school, to learn to read the laws of the commonwealth, to ripen his wits from his childhood, and so to proceed in his learning till he be acquainted with all arts and languages. And the reason is threefold:

First, by being acquainted with the knowledge of the affairs of the world, by this traditional knowledge they may be the better able to govern themselves like rational men;

Secondly, they may become thereby good commonwealth's men, in supporting the government thereof, by being acquainted with the nature of government;

Thirdly, if England have occasion to send ambassadors to any other land, we may have such as are acquainted with their language; or if any ambassador come from other lands, we may have such as can understand their speech.

But one sort of children shall not be trained up only to book learning and no other employment, called scholars, as they are in the government of monarchy; for then through idleness and exercised wit therein they spend their time to find out policies to advance themselves to be lords and masters above their labouring brethren, as Simeon and Levi do, which occasions all the trouble in the world.

Therefore, to prevent the dangerous events of idleness in scholars, it is reason, and safe for common peace, that after children have been brought up at schools to ripen their wits, they shall then be set to such trades, arts and sciences as their bodies and wits are capable of; and therein continue till they come to forty years of age.

For all the work of the earth, or in trades, is to be managed by youth, and by such as have lost their freedoms.

Then from forty years of age till fourscore, if he live so long, which is the degree of manhood and old age, they shall be freed from all labour and work, unless they will themselves.

And from among this degree of mankind shall be chosen all officers and overseers, to see the laws of the commonwealth observed.

For as all men shall be workers or waiters in store-houses till they be forty years of age, so none shall be chosen a public officer till he be full forty years of age: for by this time man hath learned experience to govern himself and others: for when young wits are set to govern, they wax wanton, etc.

What trades should mankind be brought up in?

In every trade, art and science, whereby they may find out the secrets of the creation, and that they may know how to govern the earth in right order.

There are five fountains from whence all arts and sciences have their influences: he that is an actor in any or in all the five parts is a profitable son of mankind; he that only contemplates and talks of what he reads and hears, and doth not employ his talent in some bodily action for the increase of fruitfulness, freedom and peace in the earth, is an unprofitable son.

The first fountain is the right planting of the earth to make it fruitful, and this is called husbandry. And there are two branches of it:

As first, planting, digging, dunging, liming, burning, grubbing and right ordering of land, to make it fit to receive seed, that it may bring forth a plentiful crop. And under this head all millers, maltsters, bakers, harness-makers for ploughs and carts, rope-makers, spinners and weavers of linen and such like, are all but good husbandry.

The second branch of husbandry is gardening, how to plant, graft and set all sort of fruit trees, and how to order the ground for flowers, herbs and roots for pleasure, food or medicinal. And here all physicians, chirurgeons,[11] distillers of all sorts of waters, gatherers of drugs, makers of wines and oil, and preservers of fruits and such like, may learn by observation what is good for all bodies, both man and beasts.

The second fountain is mineral employment, and that is to search into the earth to find out mines of gold and silver, brass, iron, tin, lead, cannel, coal and stone of all sorts, saltpetre, salt and alum-springs and such like. And here all chemists, gunpowder-makers, masons, smiths and such like, as would find out the strength and power of the earth, may learn how to order these for the use and profit of mankind.

The third fountain is the right ordering of cattle, whether by shepherds or herdsmen; and such may learn here how to breed and train up cows for the dairies, bulls and horses for the saddle or yoke. And here all tanners, hatters, shoemakers, glovers, spinners of wool, clothiers, tailors, dyers and such like, may learn how to order and look to these.

The fourth fountain is the right ordering of woods and timber trees, for planting, dressing, felling, framing of timber for all uses, for building houses or ships. And here all carpenters, joiners, throsters,[13] plough-makers, instrument-makers for music, and all who work in wood and timber, may find out the secret[s] of nature, to make trees more Plentiful and thriving in their growth and profitable for use.

The fifth fountain, from whence reason is exercised to find out the secrets of nature, is to observe the rising and setting of the sun, moon and the powers of the heavens above; and the motion of the tides and seas, and their several effects, powers and operations upon the bodies of man and beast. And here may be learned astrology, astronomy and navigation, and the motions of the winds and the causes of several appearances of the face of heaven, either in storms or in fairness.

And in all these five fountains here is knowledge in the practice, and it is good.

But there is traditional knowledge, which is attained by reading or by the instruction of others, and not practical but leads to an idle life; and this is not good.

The first is a laborious knowledge, and a preserver of common peace, which we find God himself acting; for he put forth his own wisdom in practice when he set his strength to work to make the creation: for God is an active power, not an imaginary fancy.

The latter is an idle, lazy contemplation the scholars would call knowledge; but it is no knowledge but a show of knowledge, like a parrot who speaks words but he knows not what he saith. This same show of knowledge rests in reading or contemplating or hearing others speak, and speaks so too, but will not set his hand to work. And from this traditional knowledge and learning rise up both clergy and lawyer, who by their cunning insinuations live merely upon the labour of other men, and teach laws which they themselves will not do, and lays burdens upon others which they themselves will not touch with the least of their fingers. And from hence arises all oppressions, wars and troubles in the world; the one is the son of contention, the other the son of darkness, but both the supporters of bondage, which the creation groans under.

Therefore to prevent idleness and the danger of Machiavellian cheats, it is profitable for the commonwealth that children be trained lip in trades and some bodily employment,-as well as in learning languages or the histories of former ages.

And as boys are trained up in learning and in trades, so all maids shall be trained up in reading, sewing, knitting, spinning of linen and woollen, music, and all other easy neat works, either far to furnish store-houses with linen and woollen cloth, or for the ornament of particular houses with needle-work.

And if this course were taken, there would be no idle person nor beggars in the land, and much work would be done by that now lazy generation for the enlarging of the common treasuries.

And in the managing of any trade, let no young wit be crushed in his invention; for if any man desire to make a new trial of his skill in any trade or science, the overseers shall not hinder him, but encourage him therein: that so the spirit of knowledge may have his full growth in man, to find out the secret in every art.

And let everyone who finds out a new invention have a deserved honour given him; and certainly, when men are sure of food and raiment, their reason will be ripe and ready to dive into the secrets of the creation, that they may learn to see and know God (the spirit of the whole creation) in all his works; for fear of want, and care to pay rent to taskmasters, hath hindered many rare inventions.

So that kingly power hath crushed the spirit of knowledge, and would not suffer it to rise up in its beauty and fulness, but by his club law hath preferred the spirit of imagination, which is a deceiver, before it.

There shall be no buying and selling of the earth, nor of the fruits thereof.

For by the government under kings, the cheaters hereby have cozened the plain-hearted of their creation birthrights, and have possessed themselves in the earth and calls it theirs and not the others' and so have brought in that poverty and misery which lies upon many men.

And whereas the wise should help the foolish, and the strong help the weak, the wise and the strong destroys the weak and the simple.

And are not all children generally simple and weak, and know not the things that belong to their peace till they come to ripe age? But before they come to that understanding, the cunning ones who have more strength and policy have by this hypocritical, lying, unrighteous and cheating art of buying and selling wrung the freedoms of the earth out of their hands, and cozened them of their birthrights.

So that when they come to understanding, they see themselves beggars in the midst of a fruitful land, and so the proverb is true, 'Plain dealing is a jewel, but he who uses it shall die a beggar'. And why?

Because this buying and selling is the nursery of cheaters, it is the law of the conqueror and the righteousness of the scribes and Pharisees, which both killed Christ and hindered his resurrection, as much as darkness can to put out light.

And these cunning cheaters commonly become the rulers of the earth, and then the city mankind mourns, for not the wise poor man, but the cunning rich man, was always made an officer and ruler, such a one as by his stolen interest in the earth would be sure to hold others in bondage of poverty and servitude to him and his party.

And hence arise oppression and tyranny in the earth upon the backs of the weak younger brethren, who are made younger brothers indeed, as the proverb is, by their cunning elder brother; and as Daniel said, The basest of men under kingly government were set to rule, who can command but not obey, who can take other men's labours to live at ease, but not work themselves.

Therefore there shall be no buying and selling in a free commonwealth, neither shall any one hire his brother to work for him.

If the commonwealth might be governed without buying and selling, here is a platform of government for it, which is the ancientest law of righteousness to mankind in the use of the earth, and which is the very height of earthly freedoms. But if the minds of the people, through covetousness and proud ignorance, will have the earth governed by buying and selling still, this same platform, with a few things subtracted, declares an easy way of government of the earth for the quiet of people's minds and preserving of peace in the land.

For as, like a tradesman, I ask the highest price:

Yet I may fall (if you will rise) upon a good advice.

How must the earth be planted?

The earth is to be planted, and the fruits reaped and carried into barns and store-houses, by the assistance of every family. And if any man or family want corn or other provision they may go to the store-houses and fetch without money. If they want a horse to ride, go into the fields in summer, or to the common stables in winter, and receive one from the keepers; and when your journey is performed, bring him where you had him, without money. If any want food or victuals, they may either go to the butchers' shops, and receive what they want without money; or else go to the flocks of sheep or herds of cattle, and take and kill what meat is needful for their families, without buying and selling. And the reason why all the riches of the earth are a common stock is this, because the earth, and the labours thereupon, are managed by common assistance of every family, without buying and selling; as is shewn how more largely in the office of overseers for trades and the law for storehouses.

The laws for the right ordering thereof, and the officers to see the laws executed to preserve the peace of every family and the peace of every man, and to improve and promote every trade, is shewed in the work of officers and by the laws following.

None will be an enemy to this freedom, which indeed is to do to another as a man would have another do to him, but covetousness and pride, the spirit of the old grudging snapping Pharisees, who gives God abundance of good words in their sermons, in their prayers, in their fasts and in their thanksgivings, as though none should be more faithful servants to him than they: nay, they will shun the company, imprison and kill everyone that will not worship God, they are so zealous.

Well now, God and Christ hath enacted an everlasting law, which is love; not only one another of your own mind, but love your enemies too, such as are not of your mind: and, having food and raiment, therewith be content.

Now here is a trial for you, whether you will be faithful to God and Christ in obeying his laws; or whether you will destroy the man-child of true freedom, righteousness and peace in his resurrection.

And now thou wilt give us either the tricks of a soldier, face about and return to Egypt, and so declare thyself to be part of the serpent's seed, that must bruise the heel of Christ; or else to be one of the plainhearted sons of promise, or members of Christ, who shall help to bruise the serpent's head, which is kingly oppression; and so bring in everlasting righteousness and peace into the earth Well, the eye is now open.

Store-houses shall be built and appointed in all places, and be the common stock.

There shall be store-houses in all places, both in the country and in cities, to which all the fruits of the earth, and other works made by tradesmen, shall be brought, and from thence delivered out again to particular families, and to everyone as they want for their use; or else to be transported by ship to other lands, to exchange for those things which our land will not or does not afford.

For all the labours of husbandmen and tradesmen within the land, or by navigation to or from other lands, shall be all upon the common stock.

And as everyone works to advance the common stock, so everyone shall have a free use of any commodity in the store-house, for his pleasure and comfortable livelihood without buying and selling or restraint from any.

And having food and raiment, lodging and the comfortable societies of his own kind, what can a man desire more in these days of his travel?

Indeed, covetous, proud and beastly-minded men desire more, either to lie by them to look upon, or else to waste and spoil it upon their lusts; while other brethren live in straits for want of the use thereof.

But the laws and faithful officers of a free commonwealth do regulate the unrational practice of such men.

There are two sorts of store-houses general and particular.

The general store-houses are such houses as receive in all commodities in the gross, as all barns and places to lay corn and the fruits of the earth at the first reaping: and these may be called store-houses for corn, flax, wool; for leather, for iron, for linen and woollen cloth or for any commodity that comes into our hand by shipping; from whence [a] particular family or shop-keepers may fetch as they need, to furnish their lesser shops.

So likewise herds of cattle in the field, flocks of sheep and horses, are all common store-houses- so that from the herds and flocks every family may fetch what they want for food or pleasure, without buying and selling.

So likewise all public dairies are store-houses for butter and cheese: yet every family may have cows for their own use, about their own house.

And these general store-houses shall be filled and preserved by the common labour and assistance of every family, as is mentioned in the office of overseer for trades.

And from these public houses, which are the general stock of the land, all particular tradesmen may fetch materials for their particular work as they need, or to furnish their particular dwellings with any commodities.

Secondly, there are particular store-houses or shops,

To which the tradesmen shall bring their particular works: as all instruments of iron to the iron-shops, hats to shops appointed for them; gloves, shoes, linen and woollen cloth in smaller parcels, to shops appointed for everyone of them; and the like.

Even as now we have particular traders in cities and towns, called shopkeepers, which shall remain still as they be, only altered in their receiving in and delivering out. For whereas by the law of kings or conquerors they do receive in and deliver out by buying and selling, and exchanging the conqueror's picture or stamp upon a piece of gold or silver for the fruits of the earth; now they shall (by the laws of the commonwealth) receive into their shops, and deliver out again freely, without buying and selling.

They shall receive in, as into a store-house, and deliver out again freely, as out of a common store-house, when particular persons or families come for anything they need, as now they do by buying and selling under kingly government.

For as particular families and tradesmen do make several works more than they can make use of: as hats, shoes, gloves, stockings, linen and woollen cloth and the like, and do carry their particular work to store-houses:

So it is all reason and equity that they should go to other store-houses, and fetch any other commodity which they want and cannot make; for as other men partakes of their labours, it is reason they should partake of other men's.

And all these store-houses and shops shall be orderly kept by such as shall be brought up to be waiters therein, as is mentioned in the office of overseers for trades.

For as there are some men more ingenious to work, so other men are more ingenious in keeping of store-houses and shops, to receive in and deliver out commodities. And all this easy work may be called waiting at such and such a store-house: as some may wait at corn houses, some at linen and woollen houses, some at leather, some at iron shops; and every general and particular commodity shall be known where they are by their houses and shops, as it is at this day. So that towns and cities, and every family almost, are but store-houses of one commodity or other, for the uses of the commonwealth or to transport to other lands.

Now this same free practice will kill covetousness, pride and oppression: for when men have a law to buy and sell, then, as I have said before, the cunning cheaters get great estates by other men's labours; and being rich thereby, become oppressing lords over their brethren; which occasions all our troubles and wars in all nations.

Come hither now, all you who challenge your brethren to deny Christ, as though you were the only men that love Christ and would be true to him.

Here is a trial of your love: can you be as ready to obey the law of-liberty, which is the command of Christ, as you would have others to obey your kingly laws of bondage? It may be you will either storm, or go away sorrowful; does not Christ tell you, that if you have food and raiment, you should therewith be content? And in this common freedom, here will be food and raiment, ease and pleasure plentiful, both for you and your brethren; so that none shall beg or starve, or live in the straits of poverty- and this fulfils that righteous law of Christ, Do as you would be done by: for that law of Christ can never be performed till you establish commonwealth's freedom.

Therefore now let it appear, seeing the child is come to the birth, whether you will receive Christ who is the spreading spirit of freedom, righteousness and peace; or whether you will return to monarchy, to embrace that Egyptian bondage still. Well, here is life and death set before you, take whether you will; but know that unless your righteousness exceed the righteousness of the kingly and lordly scribes and Pharisees, you shall never enjoy true peace in your spirit.

Chapter Six

The Kings' old laws cannot govern a free Commonwealth

They cannot govern in times of bondage and in times of freedom too: they have indeed served many masters, popish and protestant. They are like old soldiers, that will but change their name, and turn about, and as they were; and the reason is, because they are the prerogative will of those, under any religion, that count it no freedom to them unless they be lords over the minds, persons and labours of their brethren.

They are called the kings' laws because they are made by the kings. If any say they were made by the commoners, it is answered, They were not made by the commoners as the commoners of a free commonwealth are to make laws.

For in the days of the kings, none were to choose nor be chosen Parliament-men, or law-makers, but lords of manors and freeholders, such as held title to their enclosures of land or charters for their liberties in trades under the king, who called the land his as he was the conqueror, or his successor.

All inferior people were neither to choose, nor to be chosen; and the reason was because all freeholders of land, and such as held their liberties by charter, were all of the kings' interest; and the inferior people were successively of the rank of the conquered ones, and servants and slaves from the time of the conquest.

And further, when a Parliament was chosen in that manner, yet if any Parliament-man in the uprightness of his heart did endeavour to promote any freedom, contrary to the king's will or former customs Tom the conquest, he was either committed to prison by the king or by his House of Lords, who were his ancient Norman successive council of war; or else the Parliament was dissolved and broke up by the king.

So that the old laws were made in times under kingly slavery, not under the liberty of commonwealth's freedom, because Parliament-men must have regard to the king's prerogative interest, to hold his conquest, or else endanger themselves.

As sometimes it is in these days: some officers dare not speak against the minds of those men who are the chief in power, nor a private soldier against the mind of his officer, lest they be cashiered their places and livelihood.

And so long as the promoting of the kings' will and prerogative was to be in the eye of the law-makers, the oppressed commoners could never enjoy commonwealth's freedom thereby.

Yet by the wisdom, courage, faithfulness and industry of some Parliament-men, the commoners have received here a line and there a line of freedom inserted into their laws; as those good lines of freedom in Magna Charta were obtained by much hardship and industry.

Secondly, they were the kings' laws, because the kings' own creatures made the laws; or lords of manors, freeholders, etc., were successors of the Norman soldiers from the conquest, therefore they could do no other but maintain their own and their kings' interest.

And do we not see that all laws were made in the days of the kings to ease the rich landlord? But the poor labourers were left under bondage still; they were to have no freedom in the earth by those Pharisaical laws. For when laws were made and Parliaments broke up, the poor oppressed commoners had no relief; but the power of lords of manors, withholding the free use of the common land from them, remained still: for none durst make use of any common land but at the lord's leave according to the will and law of-the conqueror; therefore the old laws were called the kings' laws.

And these old laws cannot govern a free commonwealth, because the land now is to be set free from the slavery of the Norman conquest; and the power of lords of manors and Norman freeholders is to be taken away, or else the commoners are but where they were, if not fallen lower into straits than they were: and the old laws cannot look with any other face than they did. Though they be washed with commonwealth's water, their countenance is still withered. Therefore it was not for nothing that the kings would have all their laws written in French and Latin and not in English, partly in honour to the Norman race, and partly to keep the common people ignorant of their creation-freedoms, lest they should rise to redeem themselves: and if those laws should be writ in English, yet if the same kingly principles remain in them, the English language would not advantage us anything, but rather increase our sorrow by our knowledge of our bondage.

What is law in general?

Law is a rule whereby man and other creatures are governed in their actions, for the preservation of the common peace. And this law is twofold:

First, it is the power of life (called the law of nature within the creatures) which does move both man and beast in their actions; or that causes grass, trees, corn and all plants to grow in their several seasons; and whatsoever any body does, he does it as he is moved by this inward law. And this law of nature moves twofold, viz. unrationally or rationally.

A man by this inward law is guided to actions of generation and present content, rashly, through a greedy self-love, without any consideration, like foolish children, or like the brute beasts; by reason whereof much hurt many times follows the body. And this is called the law in the members warring against the law of the mind.

Or when there is an inward watchful oversight of all motions to action, considering the end and effects of those actions, that there be no excess in diet, in speech or in action break forth to the prejudice of a man's self or others. And this is called the light in man, the reasonable power, or the v law of the mind.

And this rises up in the heart, by an experimental observation of that peace and trouble which such and such words, thoughts and actions bring the man into. And this is called the record on high; for it is a record in a man's heart above the former unreasonable power. And it is called the witness or testimony of a man's own conscience.

And it is said, to the law and to the testimony etc., for this moderate watchfulness is still the law of nature in a higher resurrection than the former: it hath many terms which for brevity sake I let pass.

And this twofold work of the law within man strives to bring forth themselves in writing to beget numbers of bodies on their sides. And that power that begets the biggest number always rules as king and lord in the creature and in the creation, till the other part overtop him, even as light and darkness strive in day and night to succeed each other; or as it is said, the strong man armed keeps the heart of man, till a stronger than he come, and cast him out.

And this written law, proceeding either from reason or unreasonableness, is called the letter; whereby the creation of mankind, beasts and earth is governed according to the will of that power which rules. And it is called by his opposite, the letter that kills, and by those of the same nature with it, it is called the word of life.

As for example, if the experienced, wise and strong man bears rule, then he writes down his mind to curb the unreasonable law of covetousness and pride in unexperienced men, to preserve peace in the commonwealth. And this is called the historical or traditional law, because it is conveyed from one generation to another by writing; as the laws of Israel's commonwealth were writ in a book by Moses, and so conveyed to posterity.

And this outward law is a bridle to unreasonableness, or as Solomon writ, it is a whip for the fool's back, for whom only it was added.

Secondly, since Moses's time, the power of unreasonable covetousness and pride hath sometimes rise up and corrupted that traditional law.

For since the power of the sword rise up in nations to conquer, the written law hath not been to advance common freedom and to beat down the unreasonable self-will in mankind, but it hath been framed to uphold that self-will of the conqueror, right or wrong; not respecting the freedom of the commonwealth, but the freedom of the conqueror and his friends only. By reason whereof much slavery hath been laid upon the backs of the plain-dealing man; and men of public spirits, as Moses was, have been crushed, and their spirits damped thereby; which hath bred, first discontents, and then more wars in the nations.

And those who have been favourites about the conqueror, have by hypocrisy and flattery pleased their king, that they might get what they can of the earth into their possession; and thereby have increased the bondage of the painful labourer, if they could but catch him to act contrary to the conqueror's will, called law. And now the city mourns: and do we not see that the laws of kings have been always made against such actions as the common people were most inclinable to, on purpose to ensnare them into their sessions and courts, that the lawyers and clergy, who were the kings' supporters, might get money thereby, and live in fulness by other men's labours?

But hereby the true nature of a well-governed commonwealth hath been ruined, and the will of kings set up for a law, and the law of righteousness, law of liberty, trod under foot and killed.

This traditional law of kings is that letter at this day which kills true freedom, and it is the fomenter of wars and persecution.

This is the soldier who cut Christ's garment into pieces, which was to have remained uncut and without seam; this law moves the people to fight one against another for those pieces, viz. for the several enclosures of the earth, who shall possess the earth, and who shall be ruler over others.

But the true ancient law of God is a covenant of peace to whole mankind; this sets the earth free to all; this unites both Jew and Gentile into one brotherhood, and rejects none: this makes Christ's garment whole again, and makes the kingdoms of the world to become commonwealths again. It is the inward power of right understanding, which is the true law that teaches people, in action as well as in words, to do as they would be done unto.

But thus much in general, what law is: hereafter follows what those particular laws may be, whereby a commonwealth may be governed in peace and all burdens removed; which is a breaking forth of that law of liberty which will be the joy of all nations when he arises up and is established in his brightness.

Short and pithy laws are best to govern a commonwealth.

The laws of Israel's commonwealth were few, short and pithy; and the government thereof was established in peace, so long as officers and people were obedient thereunto.

But those many laws in the days of the kings of England, which were made, some in times of popery, and some in times of protestantism, and the proceedings of the law being in French and Latin, hath produced two great evils in England.

First, it hath occasioned much ignorance among the people, and much contention; and the people have mightily erred through want of knowledge, and thereby they have run into great expense of money by suits of law, or else many have been imprisoned, whipped, banished, lost their estates and lives by that law which they were ignorant of, till the scourge thereof was upon their backs. This is a sore evil among the people.

Secondly, the people's ignorance of the laws hath bred many sons of contention: for when any difference falls out between man and man, they neither of them know which offends the other; therefore both of them thinking their cause is good, they delight to make use of the law; and then they go and give a lawyer money to tell them which of them was the offender. The lawyer, being glad to maintain their own trade, sets them together by the ears, till all their monies be near spent; and then bids them refer the business to their neighbours, to make them friends; which might have been done at the first.

So that the course of the law and lawyers hath been a mere snare to entrap the people, and to pull their estates from them by craft; for the lawyers do uphold the conqueror's interest and the people's slavery: so that the king, seeing that, did put all the affairs of judicature into their hands. And all this must be called justice, but it is a sore evil.

But now if the laws were few and short, and often read, it would prevent those evils; and everyone, knowing when they did well and when ill, would be very cautious of their words and actions; and this would escape the lawyers' craft.

As Moses's laws in Israel's commonwealth: The people did talk of them when they lay down and when they rose up, and as they walked by the way; and bound them as bracelets upon their hands: so that they were an understanding people in the laws wherein their peace did depend.

But it is a sign that England is a blinded and a snared generation; their leaders through pride and covetousness have caused them to err, yea and perish too, for want of the knowledge of the laws, which hath the power of life and death, freedom and bondage, in its hand. But I hope better things hereafter.

What may be those particular laws, or such a method of laws, whereby a commonwealth may be governed?

1. The bare letter of the law established by act of Parliament shall be the rule for officer and people, and the chief judge of all actions.

2. He or they who add or diminish from the law, excepting in the court of Parliament, shall be cashiered his office, and never bear office more.

3. No man shall administer the law for money or reward; he that doth shall die as a traitor to the commonwealth: for when money must buy and sell justice and bear all the sway, there is nothing but oppression to be expected.

4. The laws shall be read by the minister to the people four times in the year, viz. every quarter, that everyone may know whereunto they are to yield obedience; then none may die for want of knowledge.

5. No accusation shall be taken against any man, unless it be proved by two or three witnesses or his own confession.

6. No man shall suffer any punishment but for matter of fact, or reviling words: but no man shall be troubled for his judgment or practice in the things of his God, so he live quiet in the land.

7. The accuser and accused shall always appear face to face before any officer, that both sides may be heard, and no wrong to either party.

8. If any judge or officer execute his own will contrary to the law, or which there is no law to warrant him in, he shall be cashiered, and never bear office more.

9. He who raises an accusation against any man, and cannot prove it, shall suffer the same punishment the other should, if proved. An accusation is when one man complains of another to an officer, all other accusations the law takes no notice of.

10. He who strikes his neighbour shall be struck himself by the executioner, blow for blow, and shall lose eye for eye, tooth for tooth, limb for limb, life for life; and the reason is that men may be tender of one another's bodies, doing as they would be done by.

11. If any man strike an officer, he shall be made a servant under the task-master for a whole year.

12. He who endeavours to stir up contention among neighbours, by tale-bearing or false reports, shall the first time be reproved openly by the overseers among all the people; the second time shall be whipped; the third time shall be a servant under the task-master for three months; and if he continues, he shall be a servant for ever, and lose his freedom in the commonwealth.

13. If any give reviling and provoking words whereby his neighbour's spirit is burdened, if complaint be made to the overseers, they shall admonish the offender privately to forbear; if he continues to offend his neighbour, the next time he shall be openly reproved and admonished before the congregation, when met together; if he continue, the third time he shall be whipped; the fourth time, if proof be made by witnesses, he shall be a servant under the task-master for twelve months.

14. He who will rule as a lord over his brother, unless he be an officer commanding obedience to the law, he shall be admonished as aforesaid, and receive like punishment if he continue.

Laws for the planting of the earth, etc:

15. Every household shall keep all instruments and tools fit for the tillage of the earth, either for planting, reaping or threshing. Some households, which have many men in them, shall keep ploughs, carts, harrows and such like: other households shall keep spades, pick-axes, axes, pruning hooks and such like, according as every family is furnished with men to work therewith.

And if any master or father of a family be negligent herein, the overseer for that circuit shall admonish him between them two; if he continue negligent, the overseers shall reprove him before all the people: and if he utterly refuse, then the ordering of that family shall be given to another, and he shall be a servant under the task-master till he conform.

16. Every family shall come into the field, with sufficient assistance, at seed-time to plough, dig and plant, and at harvest-time to reap the fruits of the earth and carry them into the store-houses, as the overseers order the work and the number of workmen. And if any refuse to assist in this work, the overseers shall ask the reason; and if it be sickness or any distemper that hinders them they are freed from such service; if mere idleness keep them back, they are to suffer punishment according to the laws against idleness.

Laws against idleness:

17. If any refuse to learn a trade, or refuse to work in seedtime or harvest, or refuse to be a waiter in store-houses, and yet will feed and clothe himself with other men's labours: the overseers shall first admonish him privately; if he continue idle, he shall be reproved openly before all the people by the overseers; and shall be forbore with a month after this reproof. If he still continues idle, he shall then be whipped, and be let go at liberty for a month longer; if still he continue idle, he shall be delivered into the task-master's hand, who shall set him to work for twelve months, or till he submit to right order. And the reason why every young man shall be trained up in some work or other is to prevent pride and contention, it is for the health of their bodies, it is a pleasure to the mind to be free in labours one with another; and it provides plenty of food and all necessaries for the commonwealth.

Laws for store-houses:

18. In every town and city shall be appointed store-houses for flax, wool, leather, cloth and for all such commodities as come from beyond seas, and these shall be called general store-houses; from whence every particular family may fetch such commodities as they want, either for their use in their house, or for to work in their trades; or to carry into the country store-houses.

19. Every particular house and shop in a town or city shall be a particular store-house or shop, as now they be; and these shops shall either be furnished by the particular labour of that family according to the trade that family is of, or by the labour of other lesser families of the same trade, as all shops in every town are now furnished.

20. The waiters in store-houses shall deliver the goods under their charge, without receiving any money, as they shall receive in their goods without paying any money.

21. If any waiter in a store-house neglect his office, upon a just complaint the overseers shall acquaint the judge's court therewith, and from thence he shall receive his sentence to be discharged that house and office; and to be appointed some other labouring work under the task-master; and another shall have his place. For he who may live in freedom, and will not, is to taste of servitude.

Laws for overseers:

22. The only work of every overseer is to see the laws executed; for the law is the true magistracy of the land.

23. If any overseer favour any in their idleness, and neglect the execution of the laws, he shall be reproved the first time by the judge's court; the second time cashiered his office, and shall never bear office more, but fall back into the rank of young people and servants to be a worker.

24. New overseers shall at their first entrance into their office look back upon the actions of the old overseers of the last year, to see if they have been faithful in their places, and consented to no breach of law, whereby kingly bondage should any ways be brought in.

25. The overseers for trades shall see every family to-lend assistance to plant and reap the fruits of the earth, to work in their trades and to furnish the store-houses; and to see that the waiters in store-houses be diligent to receive in and deliver out any goods, without buying and selling, to any man whatsoever.

26. While any overseer is in the performance of his place, everyone shall assist him, upon pain of open reproof (or cashiered if he be

another officer) or forfeiture of freedom, according to the nature of the business in hand in which he refused his assistance.

Laws against buying and selling:

27. If any man entice another to buy and sell, and he who is enticed doth not yield but makes it known to the overseer, the enticer shall lose his freedom for twelve months and the overseer shall give words [in] commendation of him that refused the enticement, before all the congregation, for his faithfulness to the commonwealth's peace.

28. If any do buy and sell the earth or quits thereof, unless it be to or with strangers of another nation, according to the law of navigation, they shall be both put to death as traitors to the peace of the commonwealth, because it brings in kingly bondage again and is the occasion of all quarrels and oppressions.

29. He or she who calls the earth his and not his brother's shall be set upon a stool, with those words written in his forehead, before all the congregation; and afterwards be made a servant for twelve months under the task-master. If he quarrel, or seek by secret persuasion, or open rising in arms, to set up such a kingly property, he shall be put to death.

30. The store-houses shall be every man's substance, and not any one's.

31. No man shall either give hire or take hire for his work; for this brings in kingly bondage. If any freemen want help, there are young people, or such as are common servants, to do it, by the overseer's appointment. He that gives and he that takes hire for work, shall both lose their freedom, and become servants for twelve months under the taskmaster.

Laws for navigation:

32. Because other nations as yet own monarchy, and will buy and sell, therefore it is convenient, for the peace of our commonwealth, that our ships do transport our English goods and exchange for theirs, and conform to the customs of other nations in buying and selling: always provided that what goods our ships carry out, they shall be the

commonwealth's goods; and all their trading with other nations shall be upon the common stock, to enrich the store-houses.

Laws for silver and gold:

33. As silver and gold is either found out in mines in our own land, or brought by shipping from beyond sea, it shall not be coined with a conqueror's stamp upon it, to set up buying and selling under his name or by his leave; for there shall be no other use of it in the commonwealth than to make dishes and other necessaries for the ornament of houses, as now there is use made of brass, pewter and iron, or any other metal in their use.

But if in case other nations, whose commodities we want, will not exchange with us unless we give them money, then pieces of silver and gold may-be stamped with the commonwealth's arms upon it, for the same use, and no otherwise.

For where money bears all the sway, there is no regard of that golden rule, Do as you would be done by. Justice is bought and sold: nay, injustice is sometimes bought and sold for money: and it is the cause of all wars and oppressions. And certainly the righteous spirit of the whole creation did never enact such a law, that unless his weak and simple men did go from England to the East Indies, and fetch silver and gold to bring in their hands to their brethren, and give it them for their good-will to let them plant the earth, and live and enjoy their livelihood therein.

Laws to choose officers:

34. All overseers and state officers shall be chosen new every year, to prevent the rise of ambition and covetousness; for the nations have smarted sufficiently by suffering officers to continue long in an office, or to remain in an office by hereditary succession.

35. A man that is of a turbulent spirit, given to quarrelling and provoking words to his neighbour, shall not be chosen any officer while he so continues.

36. All men from twenty years of age upwards shall have freedom of voice to choose officers, unless they be such as lie under the sentence of the law.

37. Such shall be chosen officers as are rational men of moderate conversation, and who have experience in the laws of the commonwealth.

38. All men from forty years of age upwards shall be capable to be chosen state officers, and none younger, unless anyone by his industry and moderate conversation doth move the people to choose him.

39. If any man make suit to move the people to choose him an officer, that man shall not be chose[n] at all that time. If another man persuade the people to choose him who makes suit for himself, they shall both lose their freedom at that time, viz. they shall neither have a voice to choose another, nor be chosen themselves.

Laws against treachery:

40. He who professes the service of a righteous God by preaching and prayer, and makes a trade to get the possessions of the earth, shall be put to death for a witch and a cheater.

41. He who pretends one thing in words, and his actions declare his intent was another thing, shall never bear office in the commonwealth

What is freedom?

Every freeman shall have a freedom in the earth, to plant or build, to fetch from the store-houses anything he wants, and shall enjoy the fruits of his labours without restraint from any; he shall not pay rent to any landlord, and he shall be capable to be chosen any officer, so he be above forty years of age, and he shall have a voice to choose officers though he be under forty years of age. If he want any young men to be assistance to him in his trade or household employment, the overseers shall appoint him young men or maids to be his servants in his family.

Laws for such as have lost their freedom:

42. All those who have lost their freedom shall be clothed in white woollen cloth, that they may be distinguished from others.

43. They shall be under the government of a task-master, who shall appoint them to be porters or labourers, to do any work that any freeman wants to be done.

44. They shall do all kind of labour without exception, but their constant work shall be [that of] carriers or carters, to carry corn or other provision from store-house to storehouse, from country to cities, and from thence to countries, etc.

45. If any of these refuse to do such work, the task-master shall see them whipped, and shall feed them with coarse diet. And what hardship is this? For freemen work the easiest work, and these shall work the hardest work. And to what end is this, but to kill their pride and unreasonableness, that they may become useful men in the commonwealth?

46. The wife or children of such as have lost their freedom shall not be as slaves till they have lost their freedom, as their parents and husbands have done.

47. He who breaks any laws shall be the first time reproved in words in private or in public, as is shewed before; the next time whipped, the third time lose his freedom, either for a time or for ever, and not to be any officer.

48. He who hath lost his freedom shall be a common servant to any freeman who comes to the task-masters and requires one to do any work for him; always provided, that after one freeman hath by the consent of the task-master appointed him his work, another freeman shall not call him thence till that work be done.

49. If any of these offenders revile the laws by words, they shall be soundly whipped, and fed with coarse diet; if they raise weapons against the laws, they shall die as traitors.

Laws to restore slaves to freedom:

50. When any slaves give open testimony of their humility and diligence, and their care to observe the laws of the commonwealth, they are then capable to be restored to their freedom, when the time of servitude is expired according to the judge's sentence; but if they

remain opposite to the laws, they shall continue slaves still another term of time.

51. None shall be restored to freedom till they have been a twelve month labouring servants to the commonwealth, for they shall winter and summer in that condition.

52. When any is restored to freedom, the judge at the senators' court shall pronounce his freedom, and give liberty to him to be clothed in what other coloured cloth he will.

53. If any persons be sick or wounded, the chirurgeons, who are trained up in the knowledge of herbs and minerals and know how to apply plasters or physic, shall go when they are sent for to any who need their help, but require no reward, because the common stock is the public pay for every man's labour.

54. When a dead person is to be buried, the officers of the parish and neighbours shall go along with the corpse to the grave, and see it laid therein, in a civil manner; but the public minister nor any other shall have any hand in reading or exhortation.

55. When a man hath learned his trade, and the time of his seven years' apprenticeship is expired, he shall have his freedom to become master of a family, and the overseers shall appoint him such young people to be his servants as they think fit, whether he marry or live a single life.

Laws for marriage:

56. Every man and woman shall have the free liberty to marry whom they love, if they can obtain the love and liking of that party whom they would marry; and neither birth nor portion shall hinder the match, for we are all of one blood, mankind; and for portion, the common storehouses are every man['s] and maid's portion, as free to one as to another.

57. If any man lie with a maid and beget a child, he shall marry her.

58. If a man lie with a woman forcibly, and she cry out and give no consent; if this be proved by two witneses, or the man's confession, he

shall be put to death, and the woman let go free; it is robbery of a woman's bodily freedom.

59. If any man by violence endeavour to take away another man's wife, the first time of such violent offer he shall be reproved before the congregation by the peace-maker; the second time he shall be made a servant under the task-master for twelve months; and if he forcibly lie with another man's wife, and she cry out, as in the case when a maid is forced, the man shall be put to death.

60. When any man or woman are consented to live together in marriage, they shall acquaint all the overseers in their circuit therewith, and some other neighbours- and being all met together, the man shall declare by his own mouth before them all that he takes that woman to be his wife, and the woman shall say the same, and desire the overseers to be witnesses.

61. No master of a family shall suffer more meat to be dressed at a dinner or supper than what will be spent and eaten by his household or company present, or within such a time after, before it be spoiled. If there be any spoil constantly made in a family of the food of man, the overseer shall reprove the master for it privately; if that abuse be continued in his family, through his neglect of family government, he shall be openly reproved by the peace-maker before all the people, and ashamed for his folly; the third time he shall be made a servant for twelve months under the task-master, that he may know what it is to get food, and another shall have the oversight of his house for the time.

62. No man shall be suffered to keep house, and have servants under him, till he hath served seven years under command to a master himself; the reason is, that a man may be of age and of rational carriage before he be a governor of a family, that the peace of the commonwealth may be preserved.

Here is the righteous law; man wilt thou it maintain?
It may be, is, as hath still, in the world been slain.
Truth appears in light, falsehood rules in power;
To see these things to be is cause of grief each hour.
Knowledge, why didst thou comes to wound and not to cure?

I sent not for thee, thou didst me inlure.
Where knowledge does increase, there sorrows multiply,
To see the great deceit which in the world doth lie:
Man saying one thing now, unsaying it anon,
Breaking all's engagements, when deeds for him are done.
O power where art thou, that must mend things amiss?
Come change the heart of man, and make him truth to kiss.
O death where art thou? Wilt thou not tidings send?
I fear thee not, thou art my loving friend.
Come take this body, and scatter it in the four,
That I may dwell in one, and rest in peace once more.

Printed in Great Britain
by Amazon